How to Draw
MOTORS, MACHINES
and TOOLS

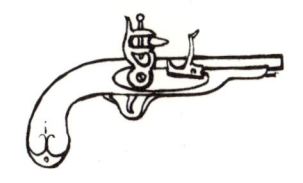

ARTHUR ZAIDENBERG

ABELARD-SCHUMAN   LONDON   NEW YORK   TORONTO

BOOKS BY ARTHUR ZAIDENBERG

How to Draw Athletes in Action
How to Draw Ballet and Other Dancers
How to Draw Birds, Fish and Reptiles
How to Draw Butterflies, Bees and Beetles
How to Draw a Circus
How to Draw and Compose Pictures
How to Draw Costumes and Clothes
How to Draw Dogs, Cats and Horses
How to Draw Farm Animals
How to Draw Flowers, Fruit and Vegetables
How to Draw Heads and Faces
How to Draw Historic and Modern Bridges
How to Draw Houses
How to Draw Landscapes, Seascapes and Cityscapes
How to Draw Military and Civilian Uniforms
How to Draw Motors, Machines and Tools
How to Draw Musicians and Musical Instruments
How to Draw People at Work
How to Draw Period Costumes
How to Draw Prehistoric and Mythical Animals
How to Draw Shakespeare's People
How to Draw Ships and Trains, Cars and Airplanes
How to Draw the Wild West
How to Draw Wild Animals

Second Impression, 1972

© Copyright 1970, text and illustrations by Arthur Zaidenberg
Library of Congress Catalogue Card Number: 73-122501
Published in Canada by Longman Canada Limited

ISBN: 0 200 71688 3 Trade
ISBN: 0 200 71940 8 GB

NEW YORK
Abelard-Schuman
Limited
257 Park Avenue So.
10010

LONDON
Abelard-Schuman
Limited
158 Buckingham Palace Road SW1
and
24 Market Square Aylesbury

an Intext Publisher

Printed in the United States of America
First published in Great Britain in 1971
Designed by The Etheredges

Contents

Frontispiece *4*
Introduction *5*
Materials *7*
Tools *8*
Basic Shapes and Forms *10*
Perspective *12*
The Hand *15*
Men and Machines *17*
Weapons *19*
The Materials in Tools and Machines *40*
Drawing Complex Machinery *42*
Speed and Power *46*
Invent Your Own Machinery *60*
Final Word *63*

racing cars

stock car

Introduction

The subject of motors, machines and tools is one which lends itself very well to the study of drawing. The intriguing shapes and forms of various types of machinery and tools are good subject matter for the young artist despite the fact that these items were developed by man for practical, rather than artistic, purposes.

Engineers and industrial designers were motivated by two factors in developing the basic tools and machines and motors used by man: efficiency and economy. Superficial decorations had no place in the efficient and economical functioning of these items. Indeed, they might serve, if anything, to impede the efficacy of the item in question and add unnecessarily to its cost.

The simple, basic lines of the equipment shown and described in this book make it especially good subject matter for the budding artist. For those who designed and developed these materials —with functional and cost considerations uppermost in their minds—unwittingly contributed to the artistic qualities of these items.

Most of the common tools in daily use today: hammers, saws, drills, planes and the like have a purity of design that most of us take for granted. How many of us stop to consider their graceful lines and simplicity? They are, after all, only "tools." The same virtues are apparent in the gears, wheels, pistons, valves and other components of most machines.

Despite the fact that these items were not designed and built by artists, they are nonetheless often works of art in their own right. And many artists today, recognizing this, are using them more and more in their own artistic compositions.

Just as drawings, paintings and sculpture invariably benefit from the elimination of unnecessary detail—and good artists consciously try to do this—so your drawings of the various tools and machinery shown in this book will benefit from their innate simplicity and purity of design.

Study the motors and machines and tools shown on the pages that follow and notice the simplicity and grace of their design. Look about you as you pursue your day-to-day activities and give special attention to any equipment that especially catches your eye. Make quick sketches of whatever interests you so that when you get home, you can develop and refine your drawings of these various items.

There is no end to the experiences that await you, as an artist, if you can recognize and react to the creative possibilities that are at everyone's disposal if they will but look for them. An alert eye and willingness to practice are all that are needed.

Materials for Drawing

Along with the countless mechanical wonders available today are innumerable new art materials—so many, in fact, that one hardly knows what to choose. Fortunately, the common, everyday lead pencil and its brothers, carbon pencils and conté crayon pencils, are still available and quite adequate for most drawing purposes.

For ink drawings, India ink and a few pens of varying degrees of thickness, as well as a couple of fine pointing watercolor brushes, are quite suitable. One of the newer products, the felt-tipped pen, is a welcome addition to the variety of sketching equipment that is available. All of the materials mentioned above were used in creating the drawings in this book.

One of the first things you should purchase is a sketch pad. You should buy several, in fact, in different sizes, so that you can begin sketching immediately. The sooner you get into the sketching "habit" the better. You will also need a soap eraser and a "kneaded" eraser, but these should be used sparingly.

Finally, you will need some drawing paper (of various textures) and a drawing board. The latter can be of wood or a smooth fiber. You should also get a couple of clips to hold the paper in place on the drawing board.

Tools

Man, in his most primitive state, found himself surrounded by elements of nature—animal, mineral and vegetable—from which he had to protect himself and which he had to use in order to survive.

Trees, which he needed for fuel and shelter, required more than the strength of his bare hands to be adequately utilized.

Rocks were used as materials for shelter as well as crude implements and weapons with which he defended himself. But man was limited in the extent to which he could shape these materials for his various needs.

Wild animals in those early days had natural weapons that

were far more powerful than those available to man. Man, however, had one important quality with which he could—and would—become master of the lower animals. He had a brain which gave him the ability to *reason*. And it was this ability that man learned to apply in order to survive and eventually master the hazards of nature.

Early man needed tools in order to protect himself against wild animals and hazardous weather. He also needed them for acquiring food. Seizing the most effective natural tool or weapon available to him, he utilized it in its natural state at first. A sharp stone, the pointed end of a broken limb or a shell served his simple needs.

Confronted with more complex problems of survival, man began to use his powers of reasoning in an effort to extend the range of tools and weapons available to him.

Fire enabled him to smelt metals and shape them into spears and axes, knives and shields.

The need for shelter and food stimulated him to contrive more complex machinery. He made saws and chisels with which to cut logs and stone. He discovered basic principles of engineering which allowed him to make levers to shift weights, and hoists to raise them. He built wooden plows and soon learned to add metal tips to the relatively soft wood to make plowing easier.

One of man's most important inventions was the wheel and it is difficult to imagine where we would be today without it. Today, machinery and tools are an indispensable part of our lives. Let us examine and then draw some—those which were used in ancient times, and those we use today.

Basic Shapes and Forms

On the page opposite are the basic shapes and forms from which all objects, man-made and natural, are constructed.

Two-dimensional
1. The circle with its variations, the ellipse or oval
2. The triangle and its dimensional variations
3. The square
4. The oblong

Below these four basic shapes are three-dimensional versions of them. They now become forms.

Three-dimensional
1. The sphere
2. The pyramid
3. The cube
4. The tube

1.

2.

3.

4.

1.

2.

3.

4.

11

Perspective

You will be making your drawings on a flat, two-dimensional surface and in order to suggest the third dimension, that of depth, you must use an eye-deceiving process called "perspective."

Notice, in the accompanying drawings, how depth can be suggested by having converging lines recede in the distance to an imaginary point at the horizon or "eye level."

In the drawing of coins on the page that follows, an illusion of depth is created by using an elliptical shape instead of the actual shape of the coin.

Above eye level, the underside of the coin is visible. Below eye level, the top surface of the coin is visible. And directly *at* eye level, only an oblong that suggests the edge of the coin can be seen, with neither the top nor bottom surfaces visible.

horizon line

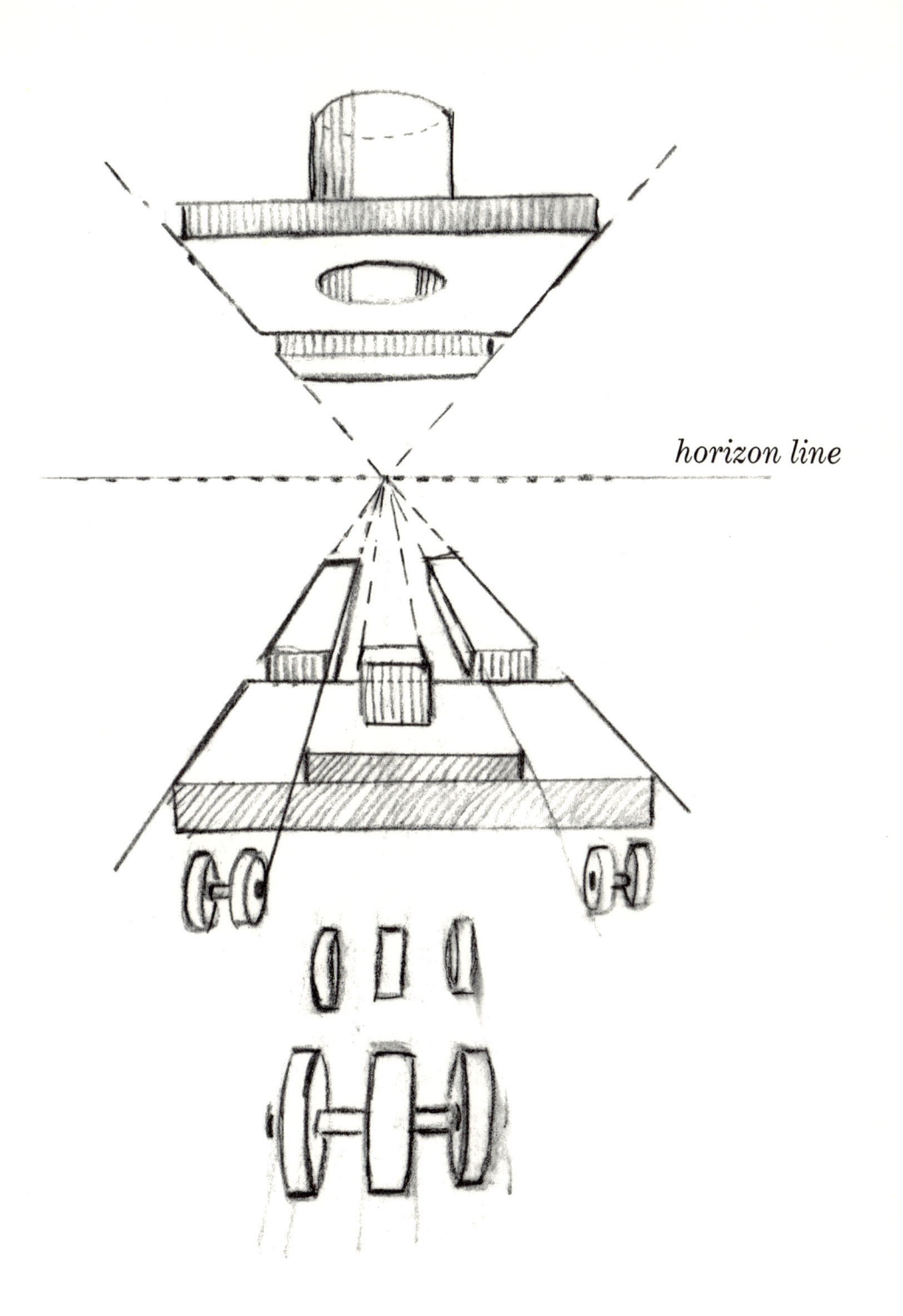

14

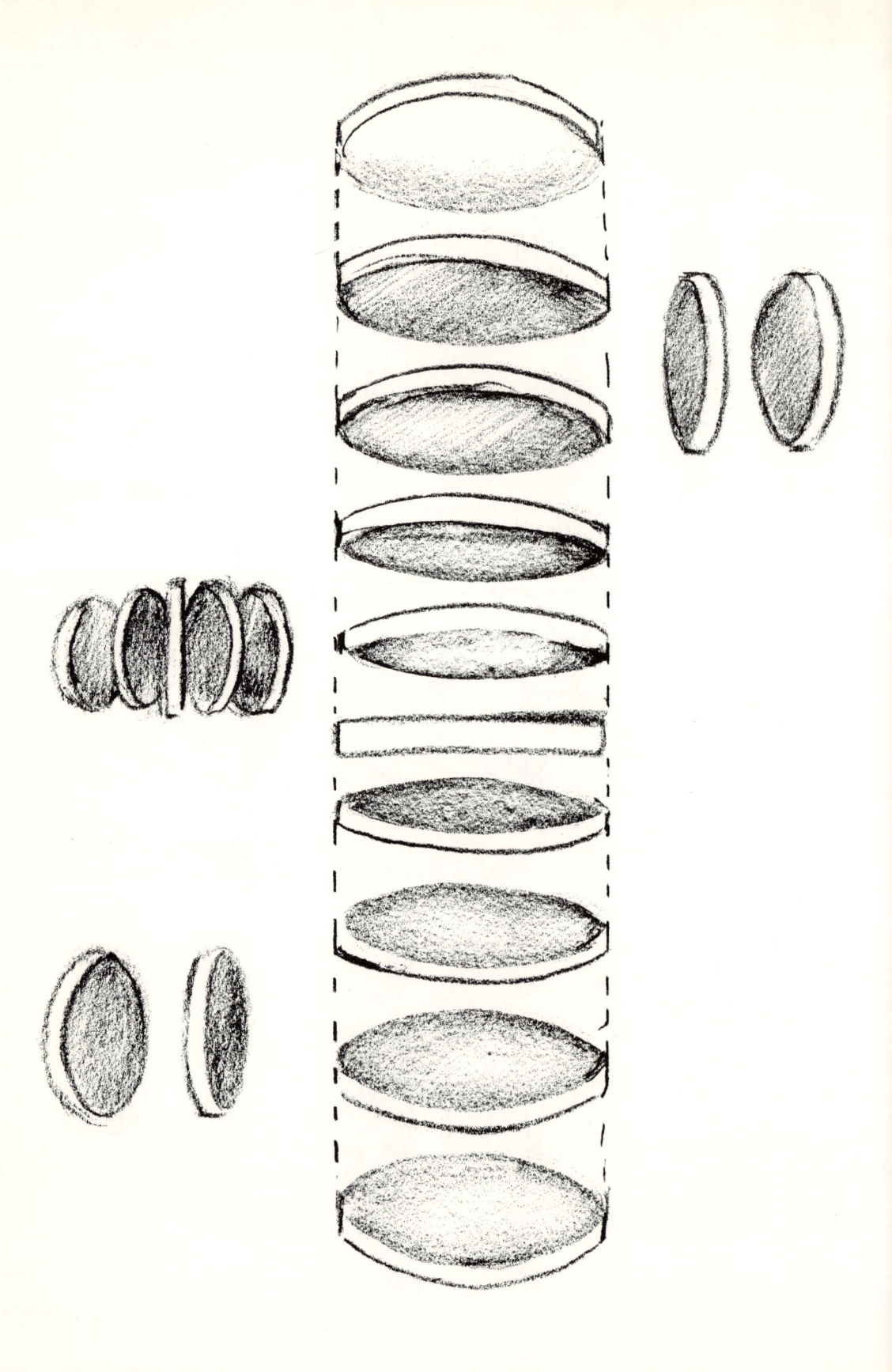

The Hand

By far, the most versatile tool man possesses is his hand. No tool or machine or any possible combination of the two can match the subtle range of the human hand.

Look at your own hand, for example. Move it about in different directions, changing the position of your fingers as you do. Touch and lift things about you and, familiar as your hand is to you, you will marvel anew at its sensitivity and incredible dexterity. Guided by the brain, the human hand has enabled man to conquer the animal world and harness the forces of nature.

The greatest single virtue of the human hand, that which separates it from the "hands" of animals (except those of apes), is the *apposite* thumb. Notice the part played by the thumb in the countless movements of which the hand is capable. It is that *apposition* which allows man to play the most subtle musical instrument or to grip and manipulate a powerful tool—to caress a loved one tenderly or to strike something violently.

All hand tools that are made of metal or other sturdy materials serve to increase the power and extend the range of action of the fingers and thumb.

Study the basic drawings on the next page and then make sketches of your own hands performing some of the activities you normally participate in. Practice drawing your hands, and those of others, holding and using simple tools. The more you practice, the better your drawings will be.

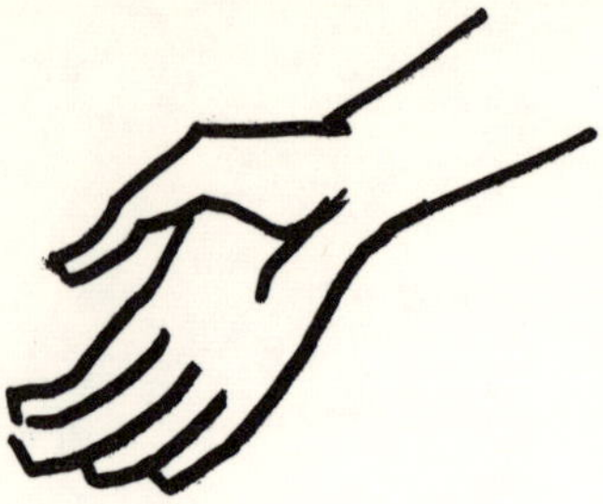

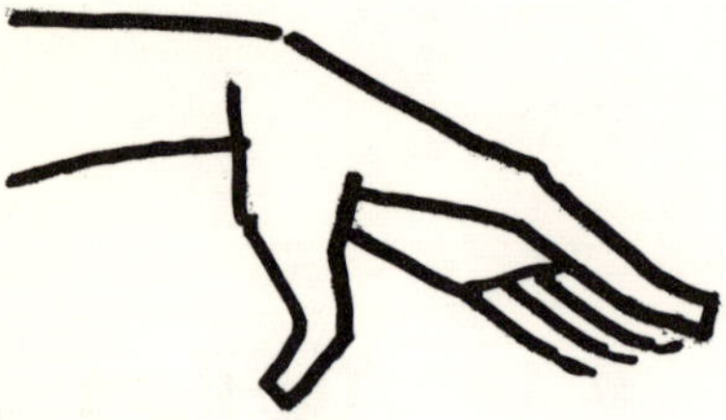

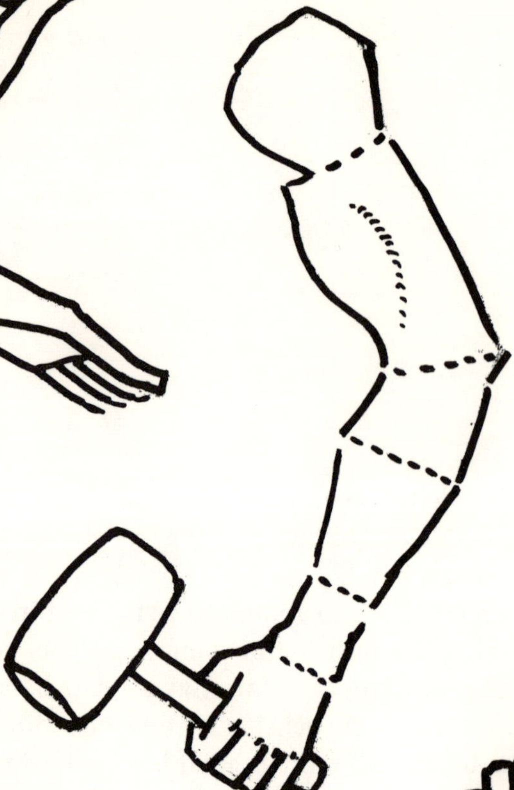

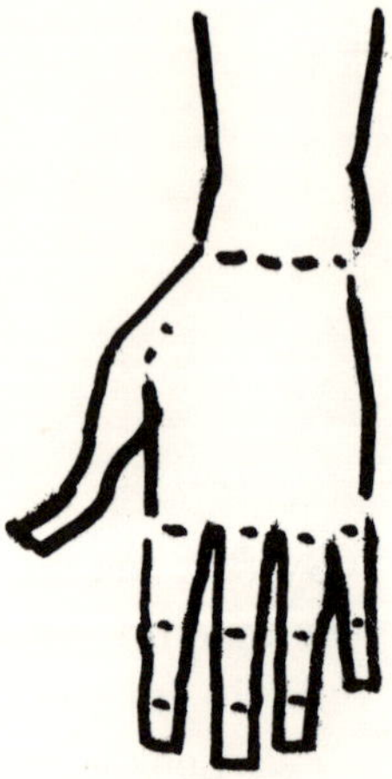

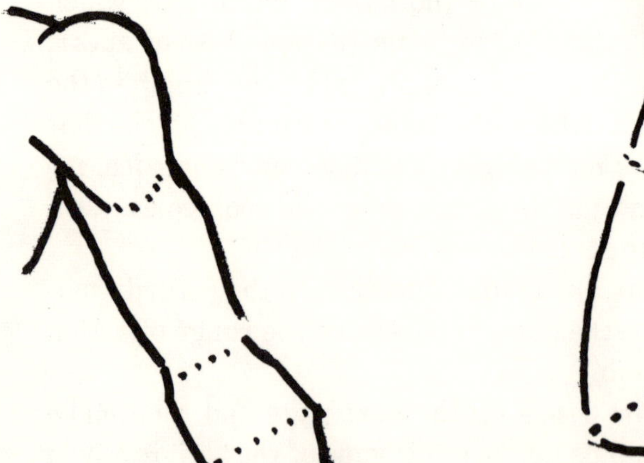

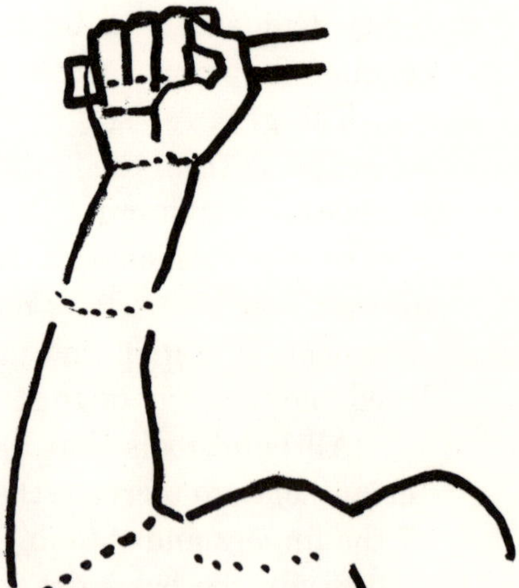

Men and Machines

Hand tools are helpless pieces of metal without the motivating power of man. In order to be able to draw people using such tools, you must study the human body and learn how to draw figures in different positions.

The drawings on the following page show the basic structure of the human body and how it appears performing certain functions with tools.

Because the human body is by far the most complex of machines, these pages cannot hope to explore the vast range of its action possibilities. For our purposes, however, this is not necessary.

There are some gestures and muscular movements that are typical as man uses certain tools, and we can familiarize ourselves with, and learn to sketch, these particular actions. The more we practice, of course, the more effective our drawings will be.

Try, as you draw, to find the *essence of the action* of hammering, sawing, drilling, or whatever it may be that you are depicting. Then draw that action, and the tools being used to perform it, with directness and economy of line.

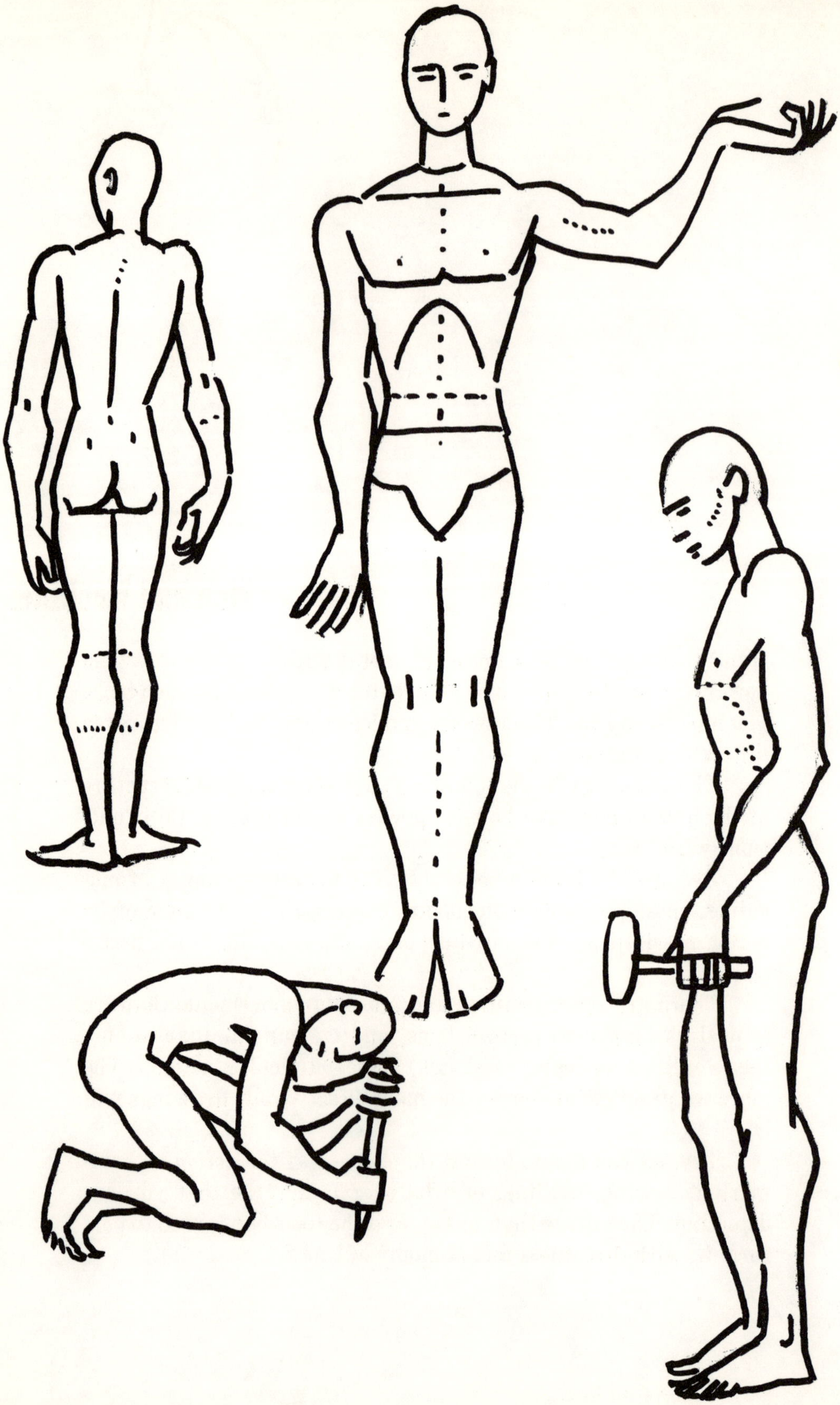

battle-ax

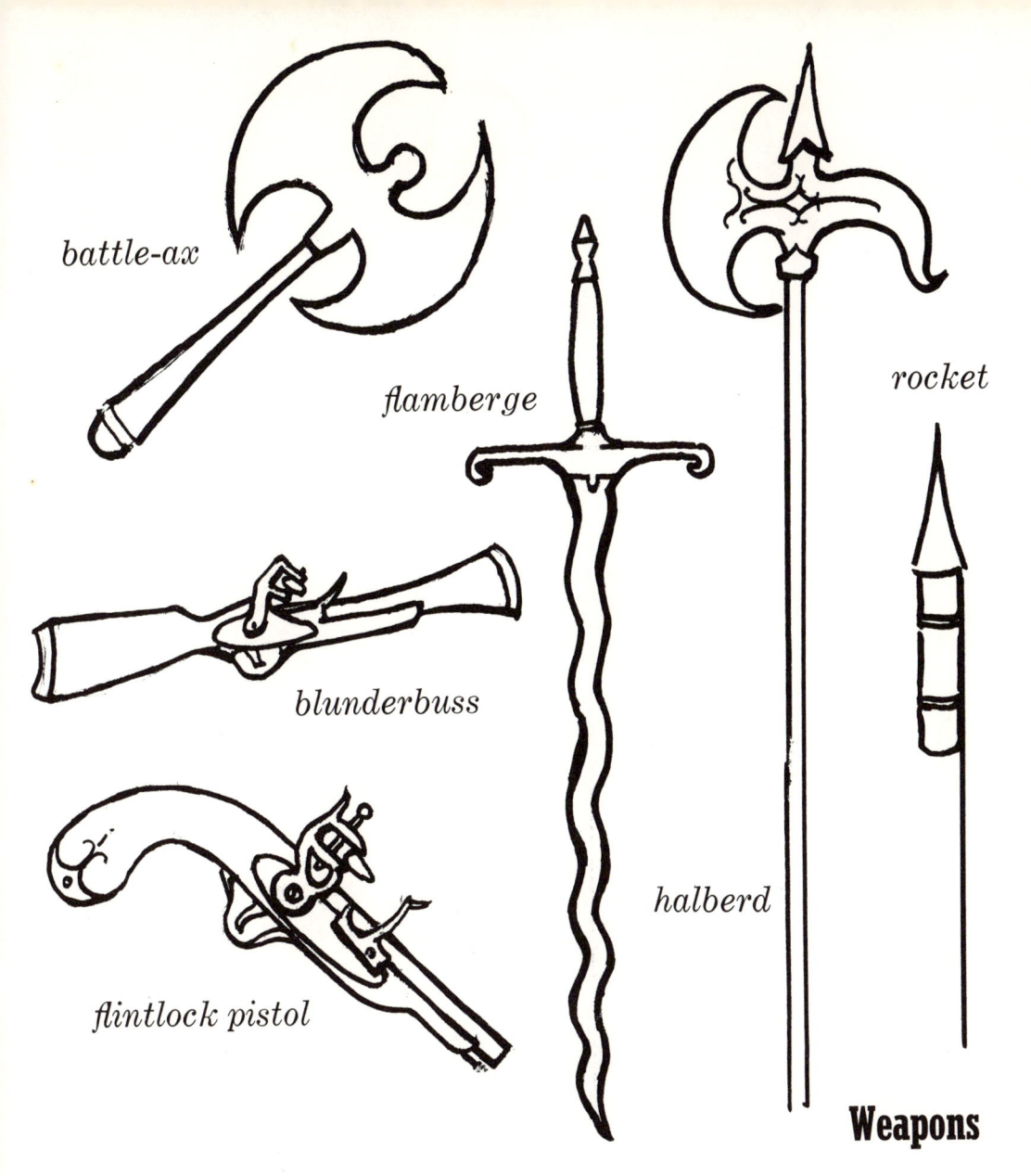

flamberge

rocket

blunderbuss

flintlock pistol

halberd

Weapons

Much of man's ingenuity in inventing things has been devoted to creating and developing weapons, unfortunately. At first, these were needed to help primitive man in his battle for survival against the huge and powerful beasts that confronted him.

As tribal wars began to take place, it became imperative for man to develop weapons with which he could effectively compete against his adversaries.

Here are some of the early weapons that were used. As you can see, they are remarkably inventive.

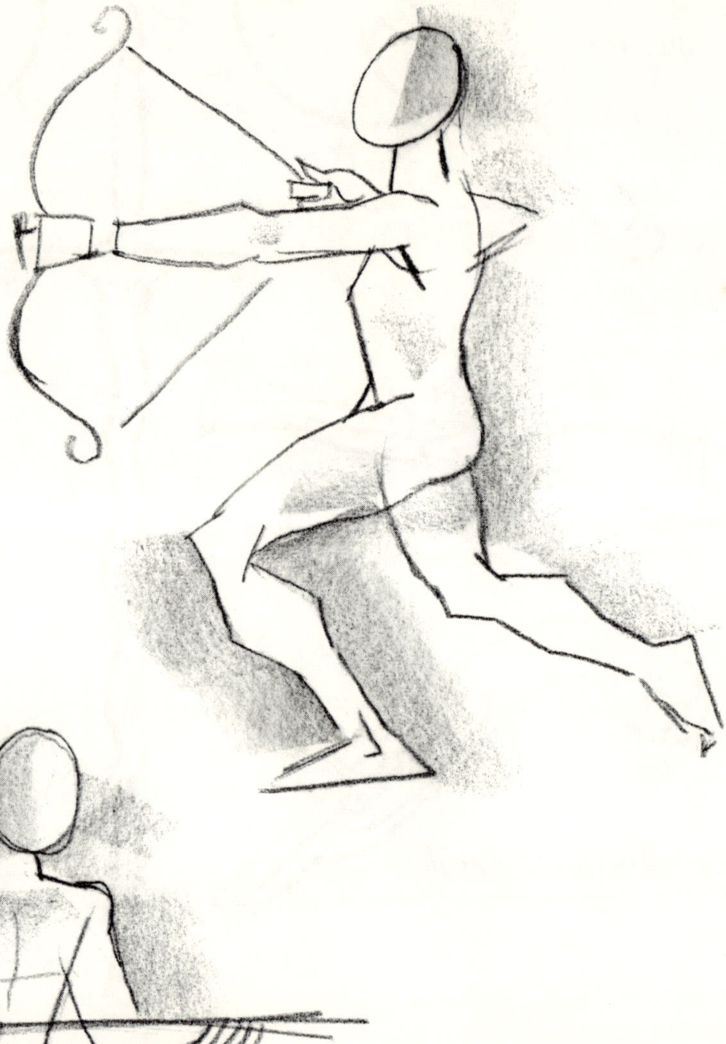

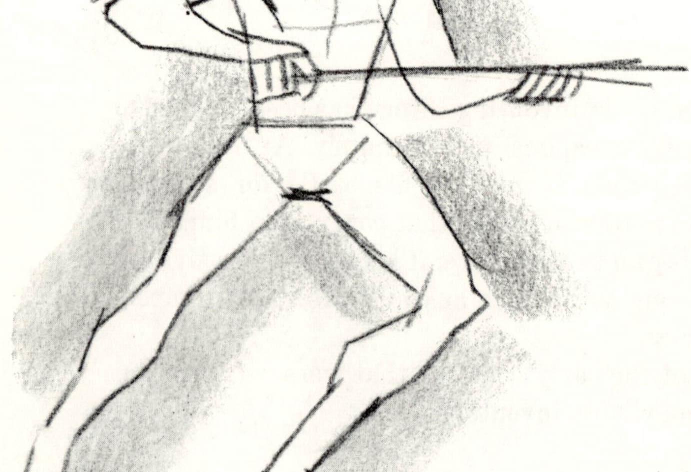

Greek bowman

medieval crossbowman

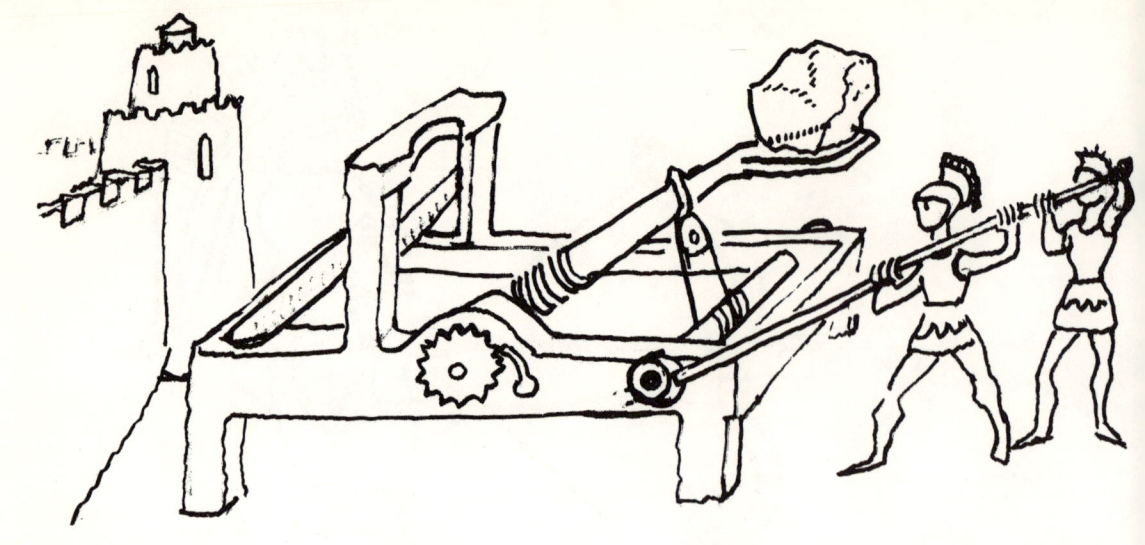

Roman siege catapult

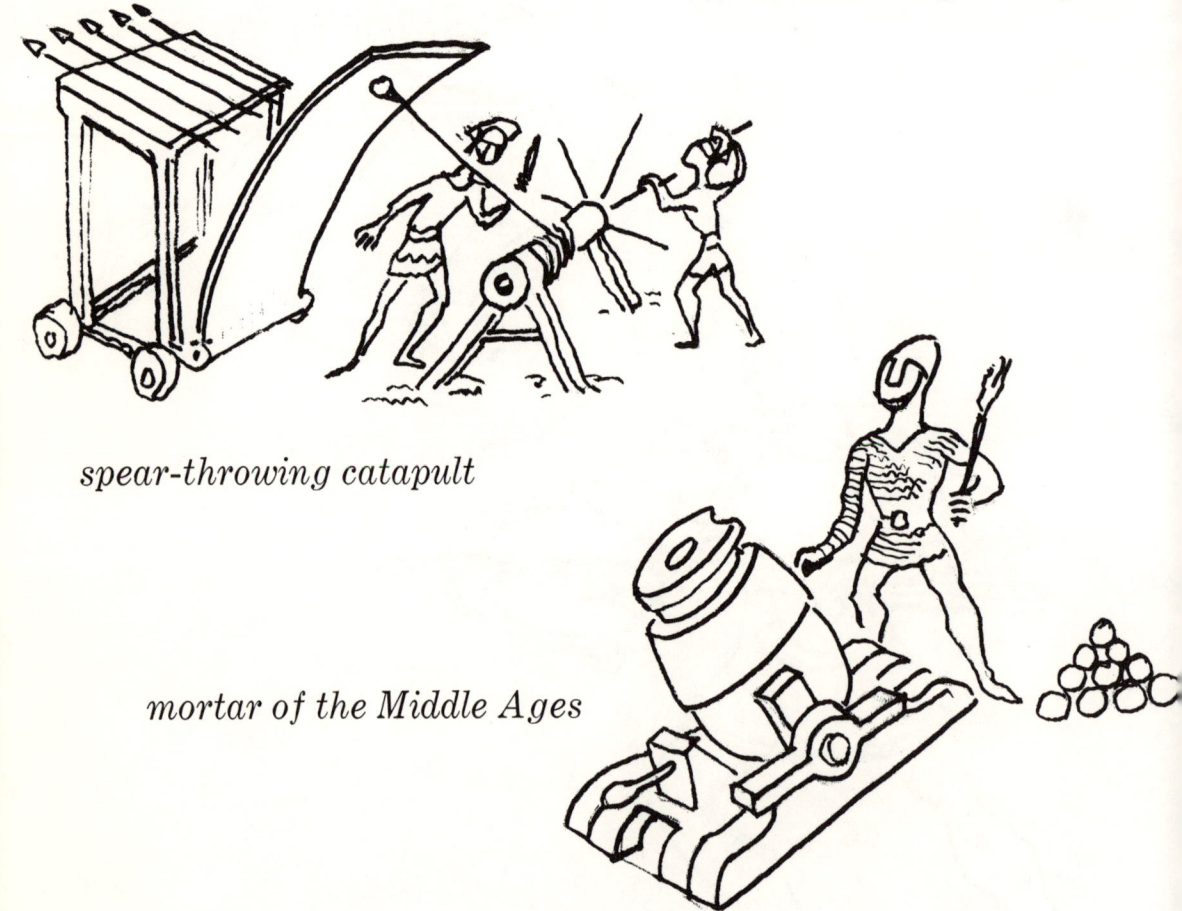

spear-throwing catapult

mortar of the Middle Ages

Throughout all the years of man's existence, he has continued to search for new materials with which he could fashion more effective tools and weapons for his needs.

bronze bowdrill from Ancient Egypt

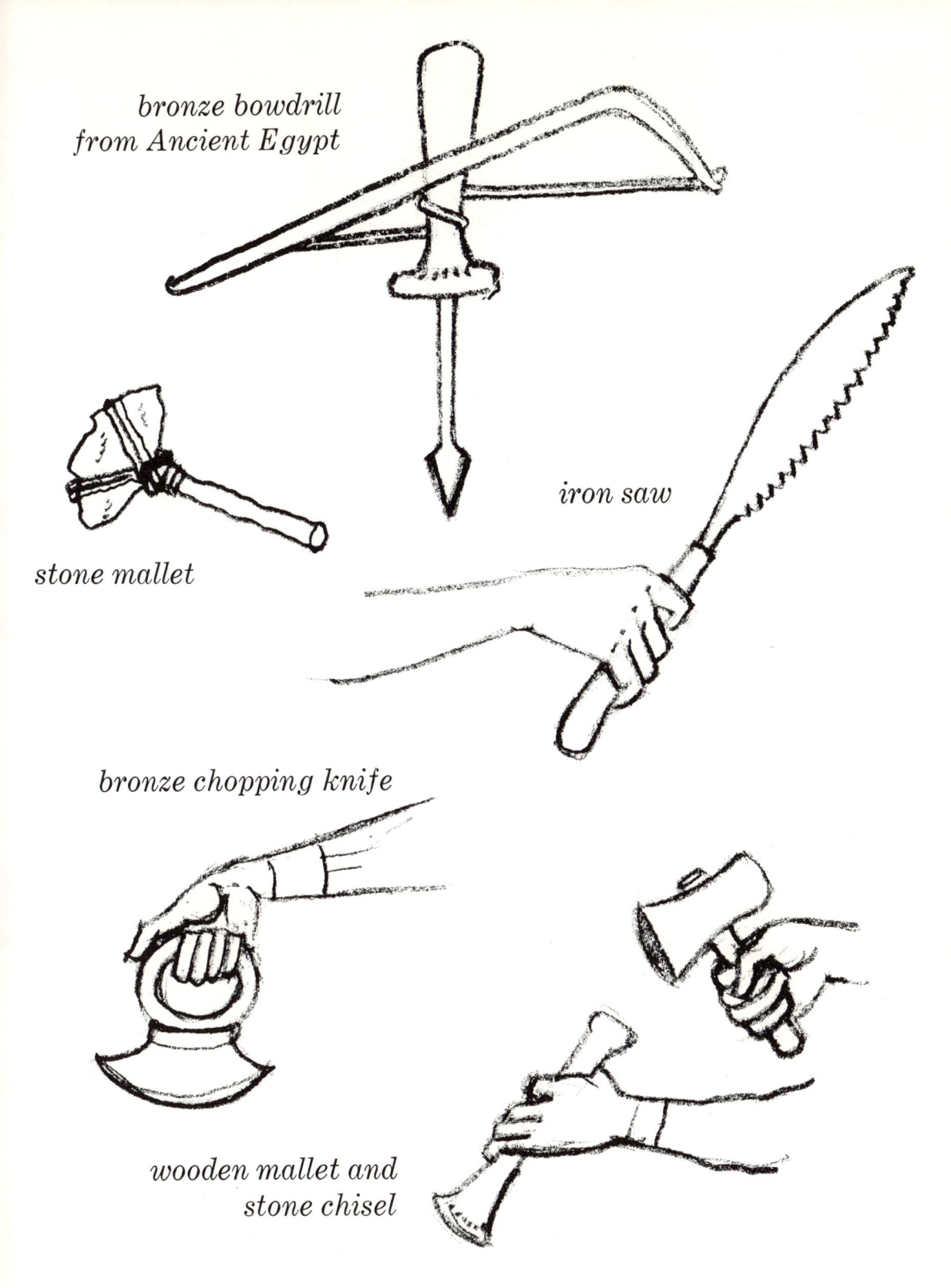

stone mallet

iron saw

bronze chopping knife

wooden mallet and stone chisel

Early man developed crude hoes, made of wood, with which to scrape the earth for planting.

Many farmers in underdeveloped parts of the world still use crude wooden plows to till the soil.

Egyptian scales

Traders and artists required inventions and new tools for their special purposes.

Greek vase craftsman

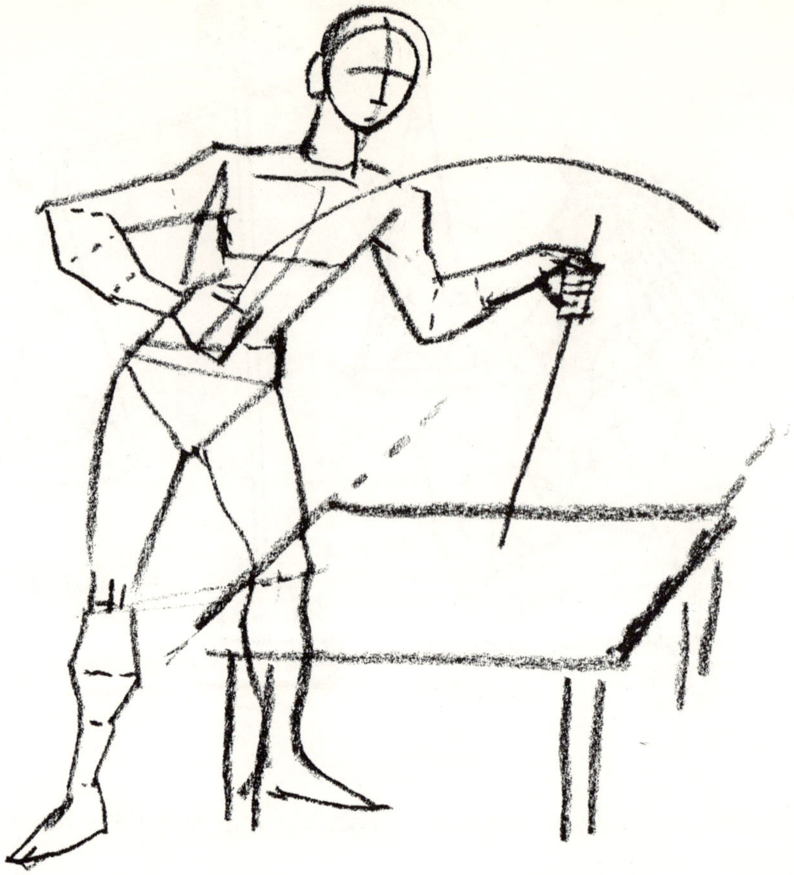

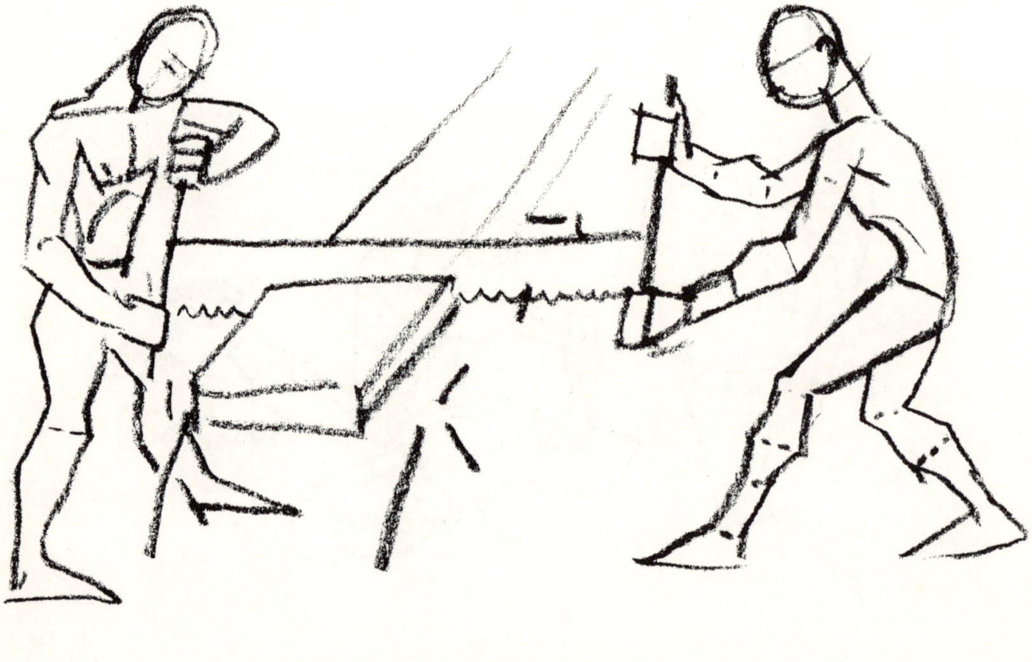

Roman drill

two-man saw

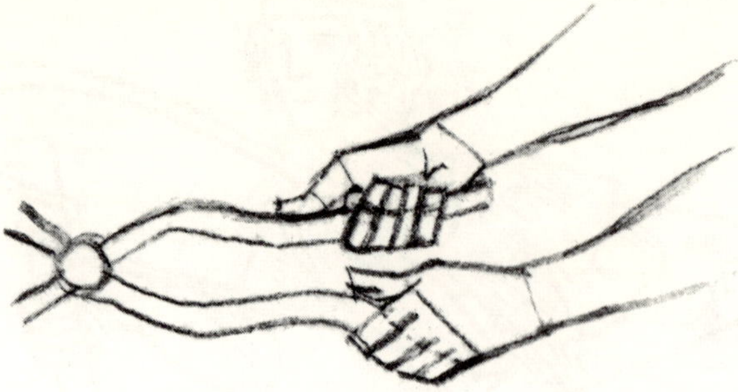

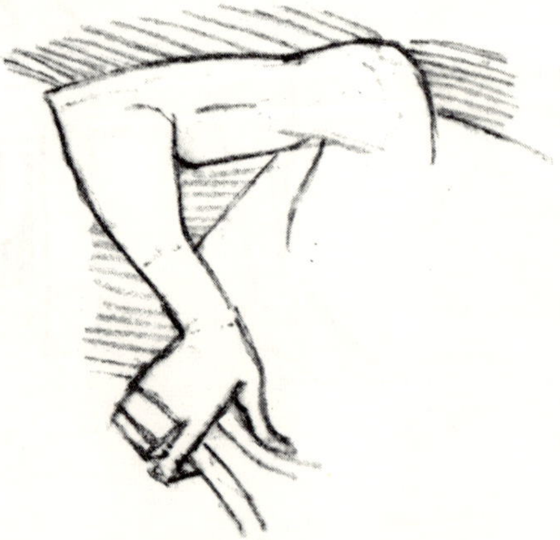

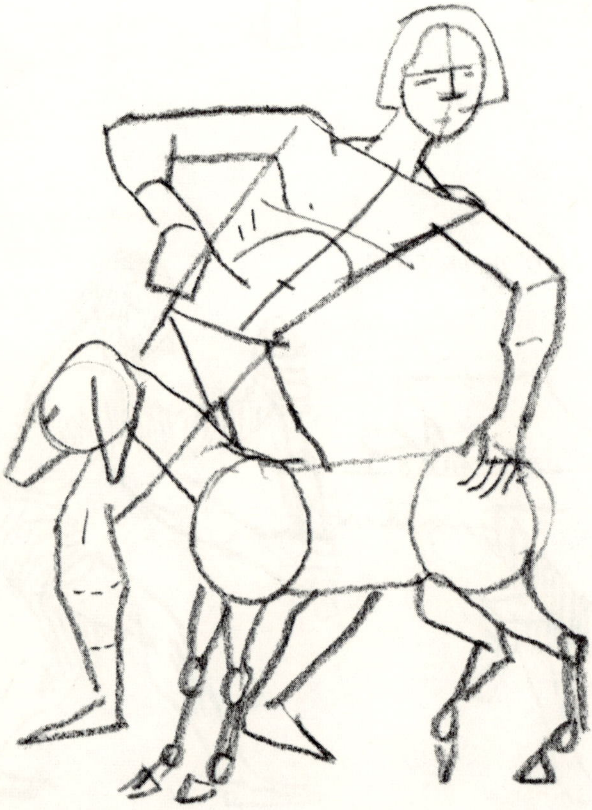

tongs

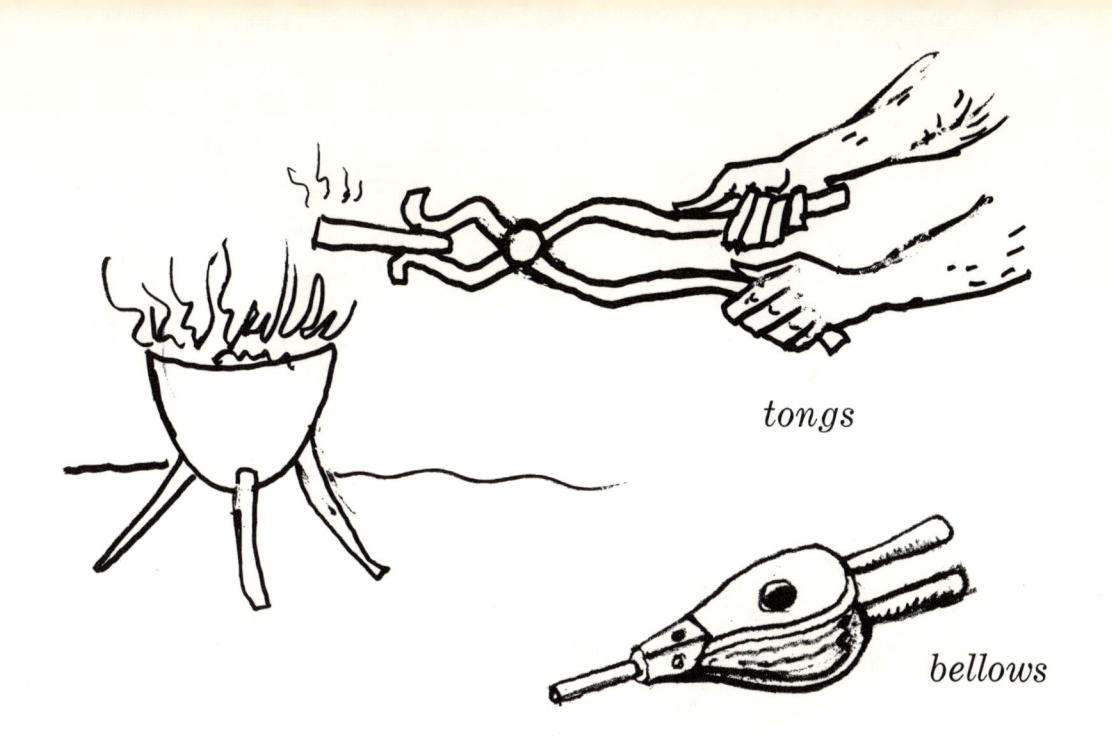

bellows

shears

Shearing tools were needed for providing wool for weaving and spinning.

spinning wheel

weaving loom

an ancient post-windmill

grindstones

early printing press

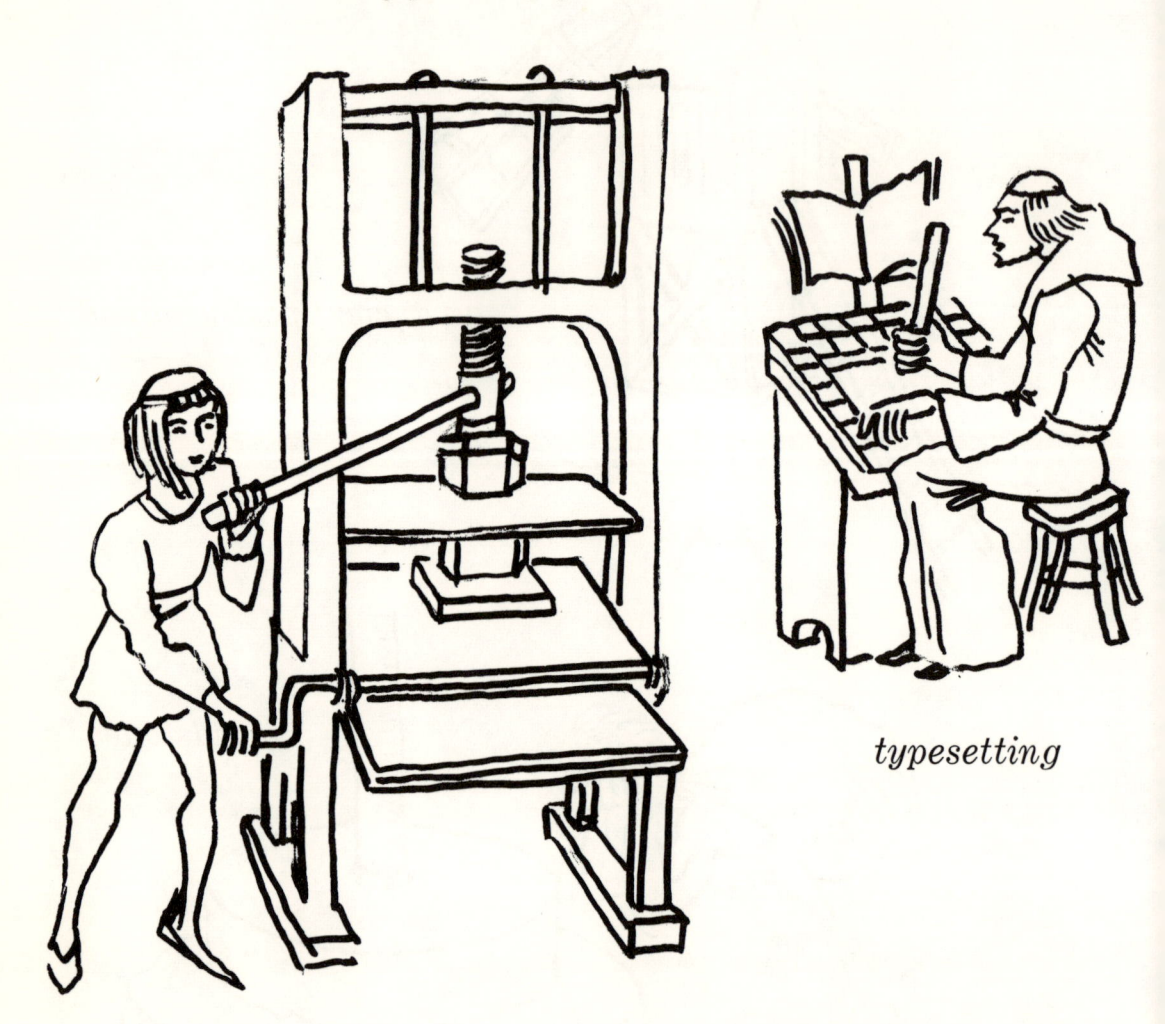

typesetting

The invention of the printing press, with its method of casting metal type, was a great step forward for civilization.

Most Machines Work on Simple Physical Principles

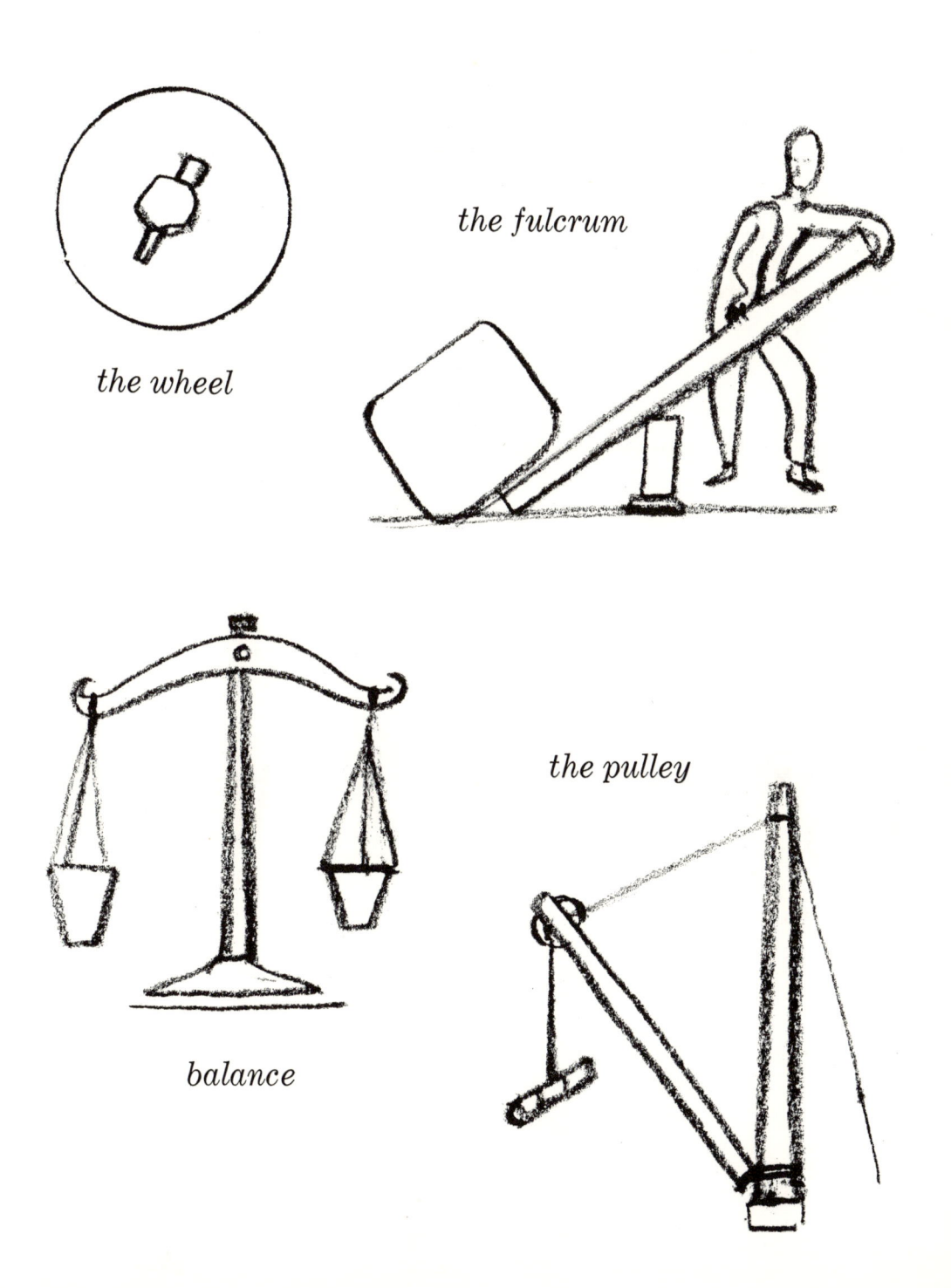

the wheel

the fulcrum

balance

the pulley

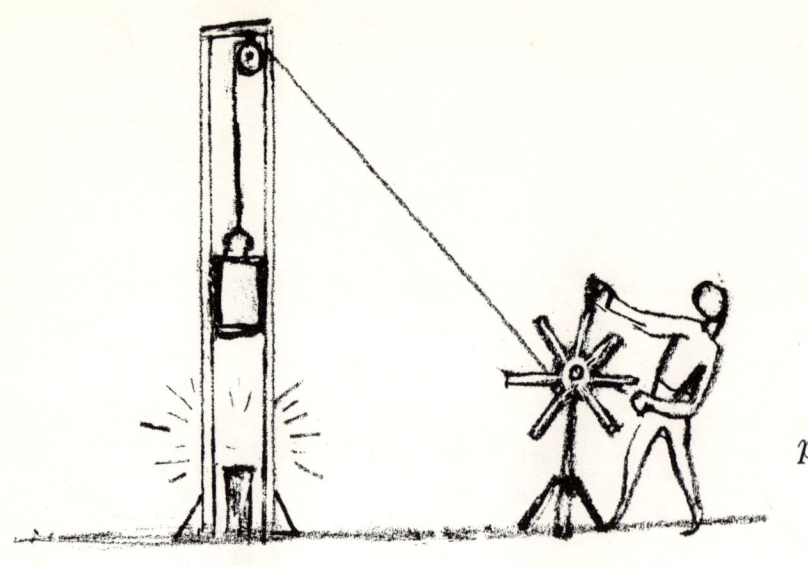

pile driver

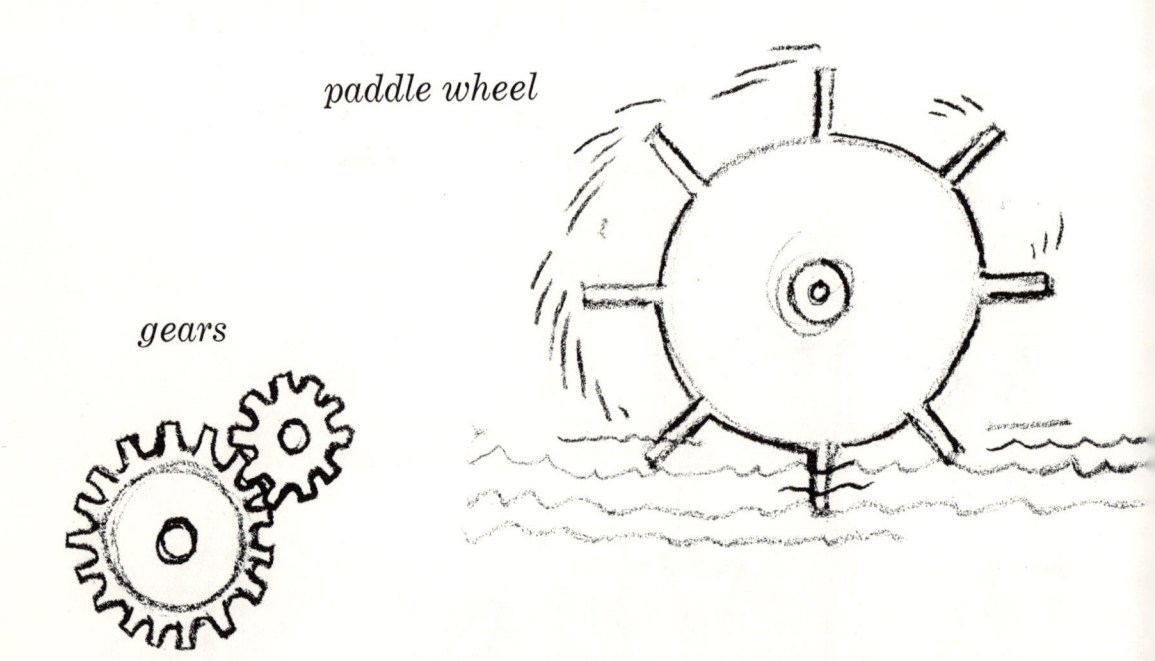

paddle wheel

gears

power transmission by leather belts

34

glider

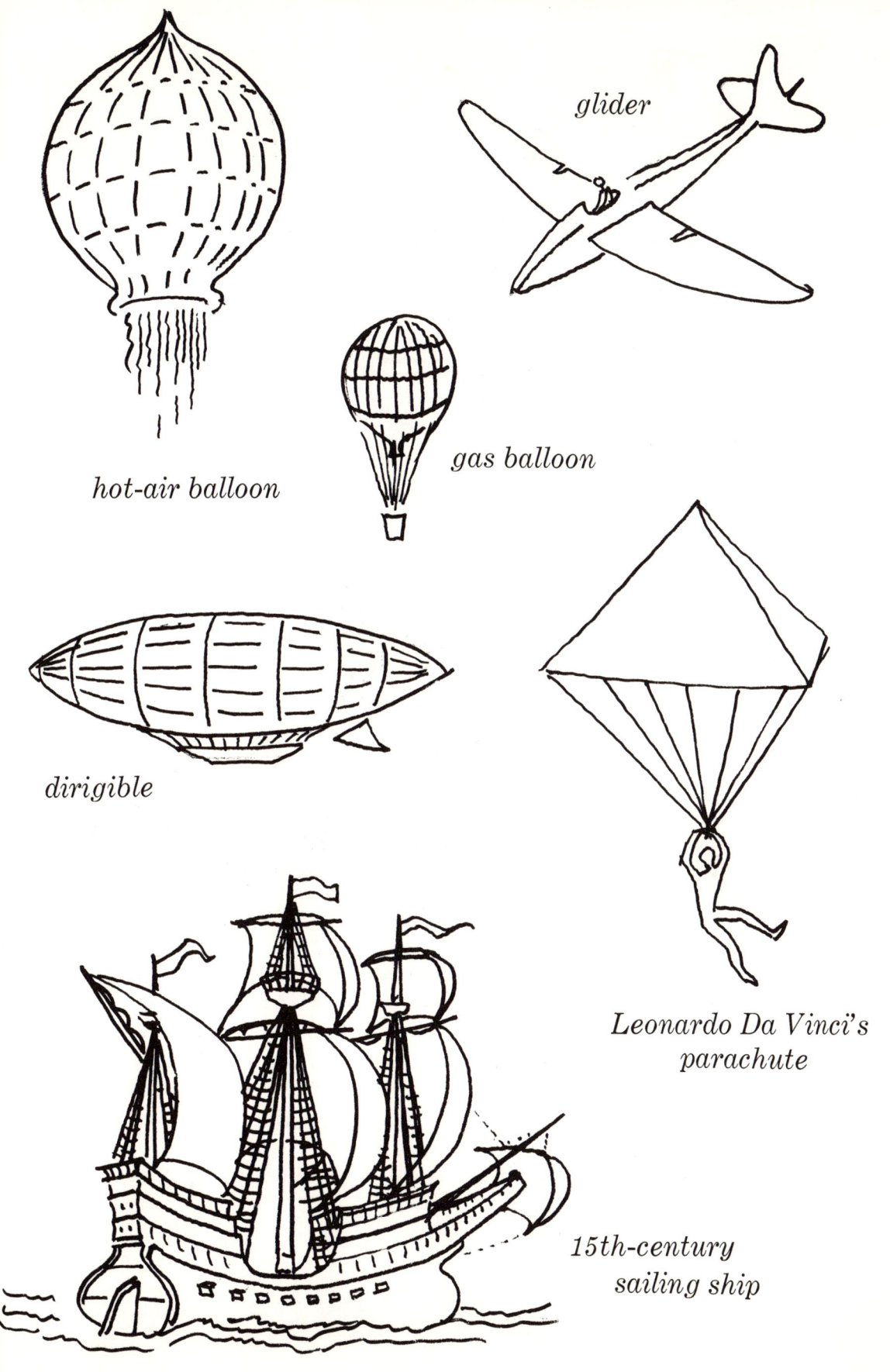

hot-air balloon

gas balloon

dirigible

Leonardo Da Vinci's parachute

15th-century sailing ship

hard material

brittle material

The search for harder and more durable materials has preoccupied chemists and metallurgists from ancient times to the present.

From the ancient smiths, who made fine swords and armor, to present-day researchers seeking metals capable of withstanding the intense heat encountered in rocket flight, man's continual efforts to seek new and better ways of doing things have been unrelenting and the rewards great.

These drawings show some of the problems with which metallurgists must deal.

tensile strength

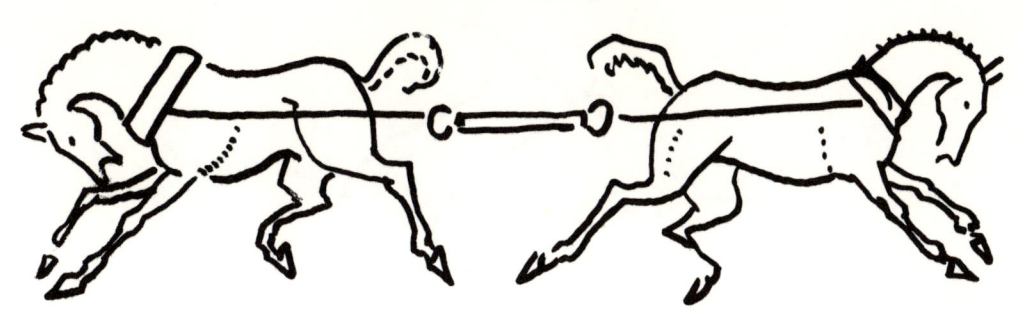

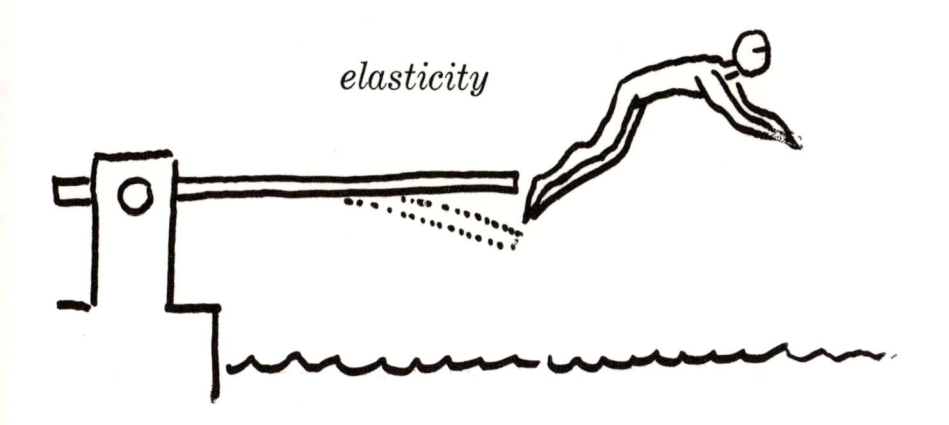

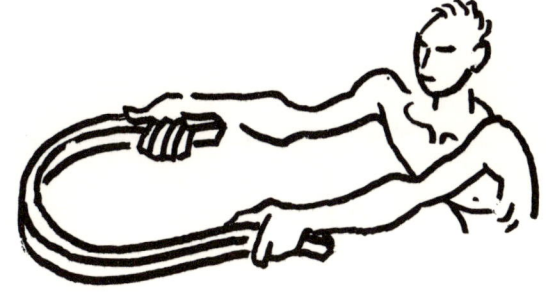

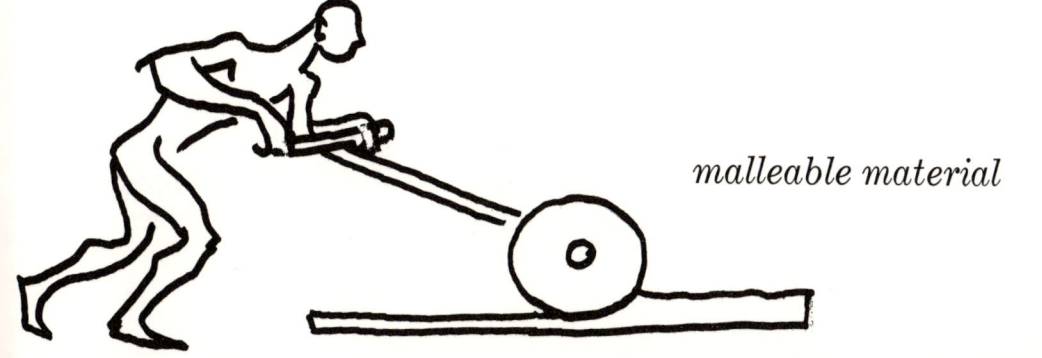

elasticity

ductile material

malleable material

plane

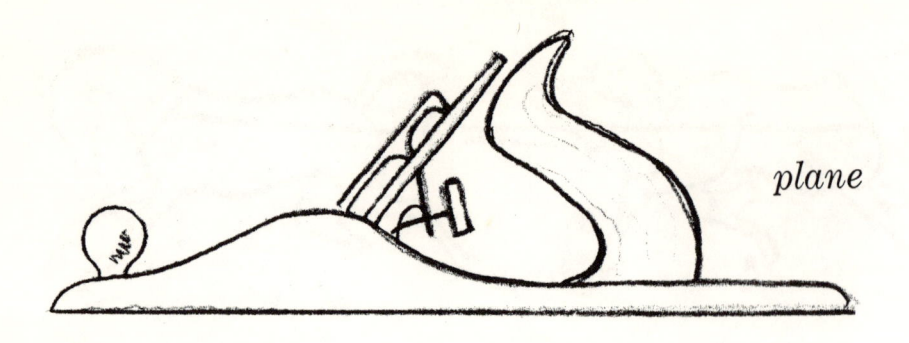

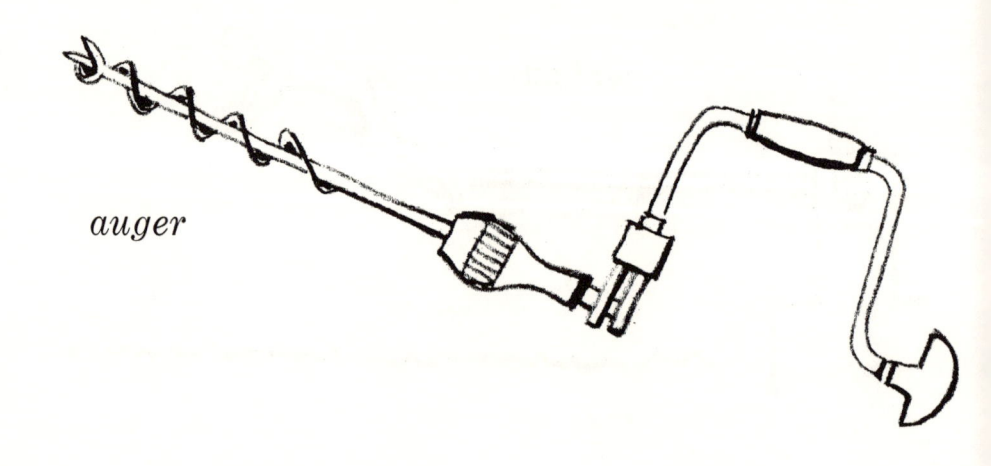

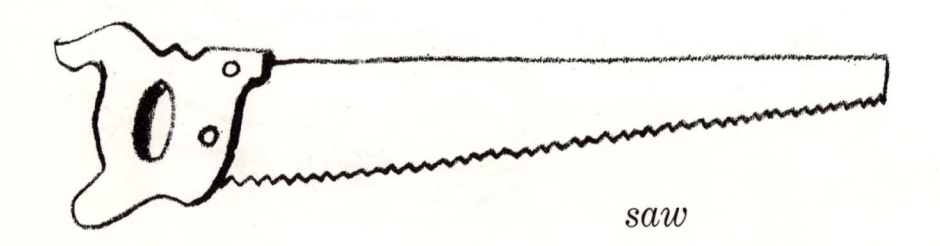

auger

saw

When man learned how to make steel (which could be hardened and sharpened to a far greater degree than iron), he developed techniques for manufacturing fine precision tools and machines.

tank, World War I

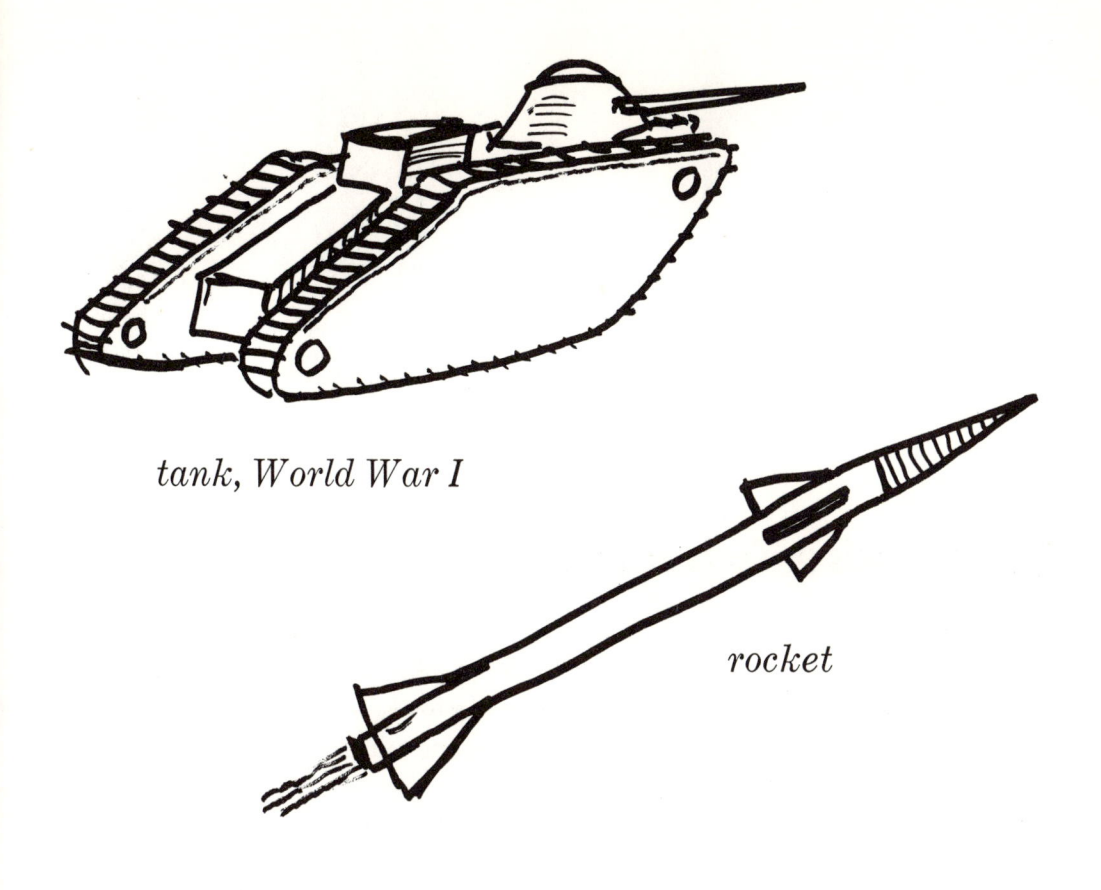

rocket

Along with the invention of fine precision tools and machines came these newly perfected weapons of mass destruction.

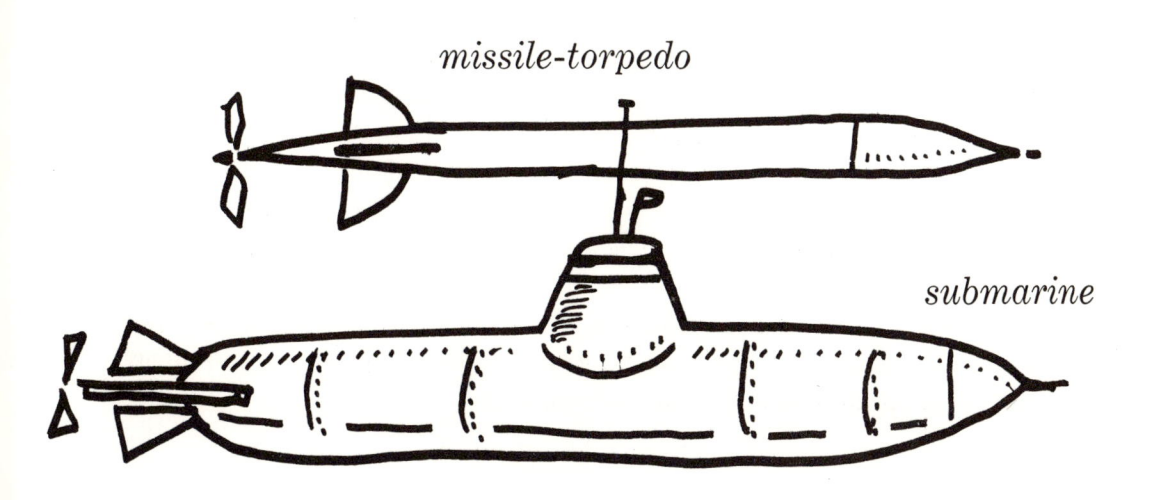

missile-torpedo

submarine

The Materials in Tools and Machines

The materials of which most tools and machines are made must be of a strong and durable nature, of course. The individuals who developed these items and the manufacturers who produced them in large quantities needed minerals, stone and wood of the toughest and most durable quality available.

In time, man learned to intensify this strength and durability even further through the use of alloys, the tempering of steel and the development of principles that would add functional strength to the mechanical action of the tools in question.

Lubrication, to facilitate the effective operation of these items and prolong their life expectancy, was introduced along with other techniques for improving their efficiency. The new products manufactured were not only made stronger and more durable but their exterior design was also improved and streamlined so that they were pleasant to look at, as well as functional.

Today, the machines and tools we see and use are made of such materials as stainless steel, aluminum and copper. Many are also made of synthetic materials such as Bakelite and other plastics. In the case of fine watches and many precision tools, diamonds, rubies, and other very hard precious and semiprecious stones are used.

In drawing some of the intricate machines used by man today, observe the purity and grace of their lines and try to incorporate these qualities in your sketches.

locomotive

first Ford

racing car

Drawing Complex Machinery

The art student in a "life" drawing class should, in drawing the human figure, seek out the most descriptive features of that figure and eliminate details which do not contribute to what he is trying to express.

Any attempt at drawing the surface expression of such things as the countless muscles, tendons, veins and bones in the human body would not only waste the artist's time in irrelevant, boring work, but it would also result in bad art.

The same principle applies in drawing highly complex machinery such as motors for automobiles, planes or even power tools. Since your drawings of motor engines are not meant to be guides for the repairman but rather, artistic simulations of the strength, speed and beauty of these powerful instruments, you should seek out the essential structure of a motor as you attempt to draw it. Try to capture the dynamic lines and major forms that will most effectively convey its potential power.

Learning to search for, and discover, these essential features is a very important aspect of your studies as an artist. You will soon be able to weed out extraneous details that contribute nothing to your drawing and concentrate instead on the character of the main forms and the total architectural design.

Study the engines shown on the pages that follow. Then try to draw them, concentrating on their essential features as described above. You will want to draw others, too, of course, that you feel are good subjects for your artistic efforts.

One of the Many Types of Auto Engines

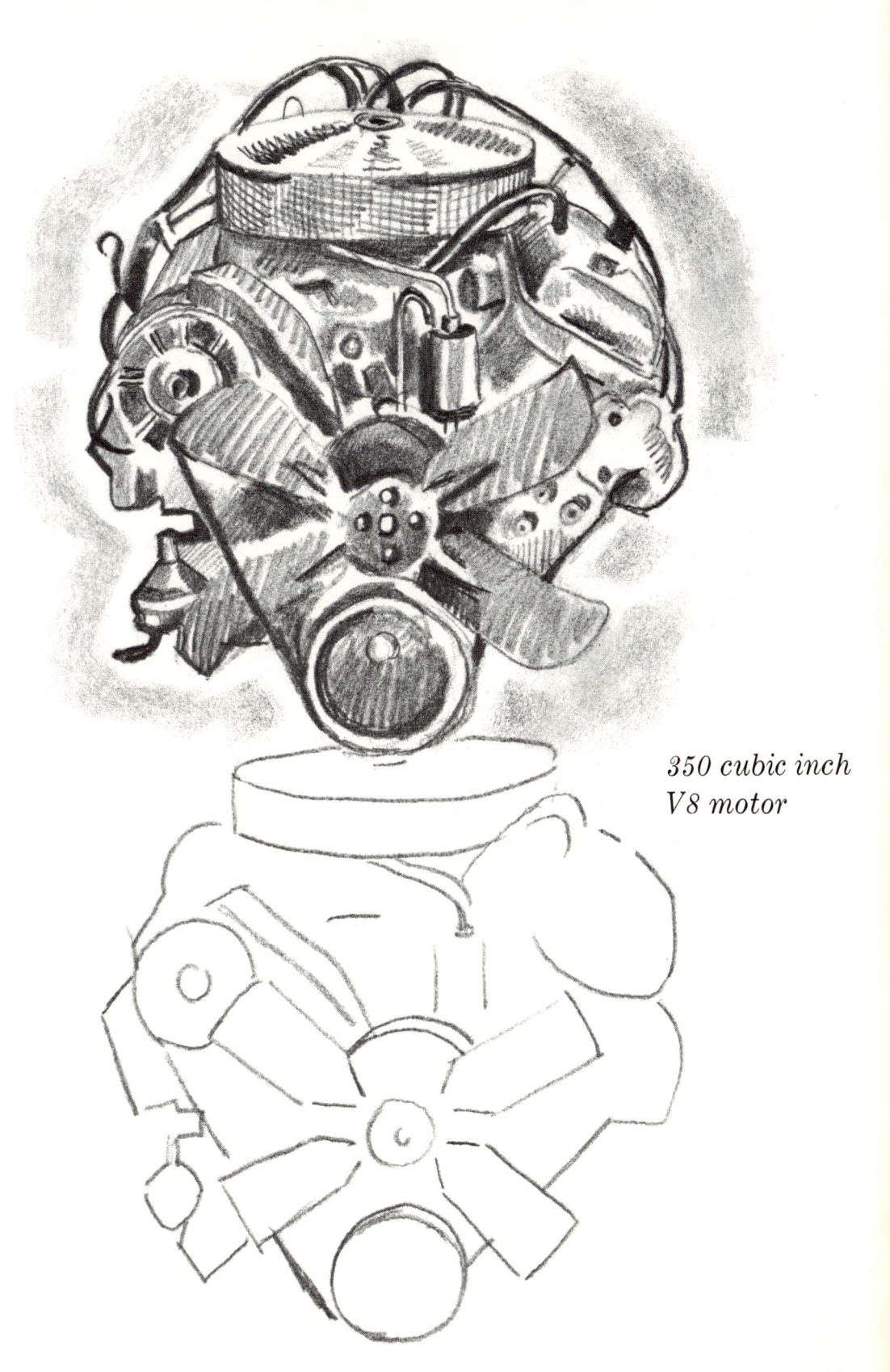

350 cubic inch V8 motor

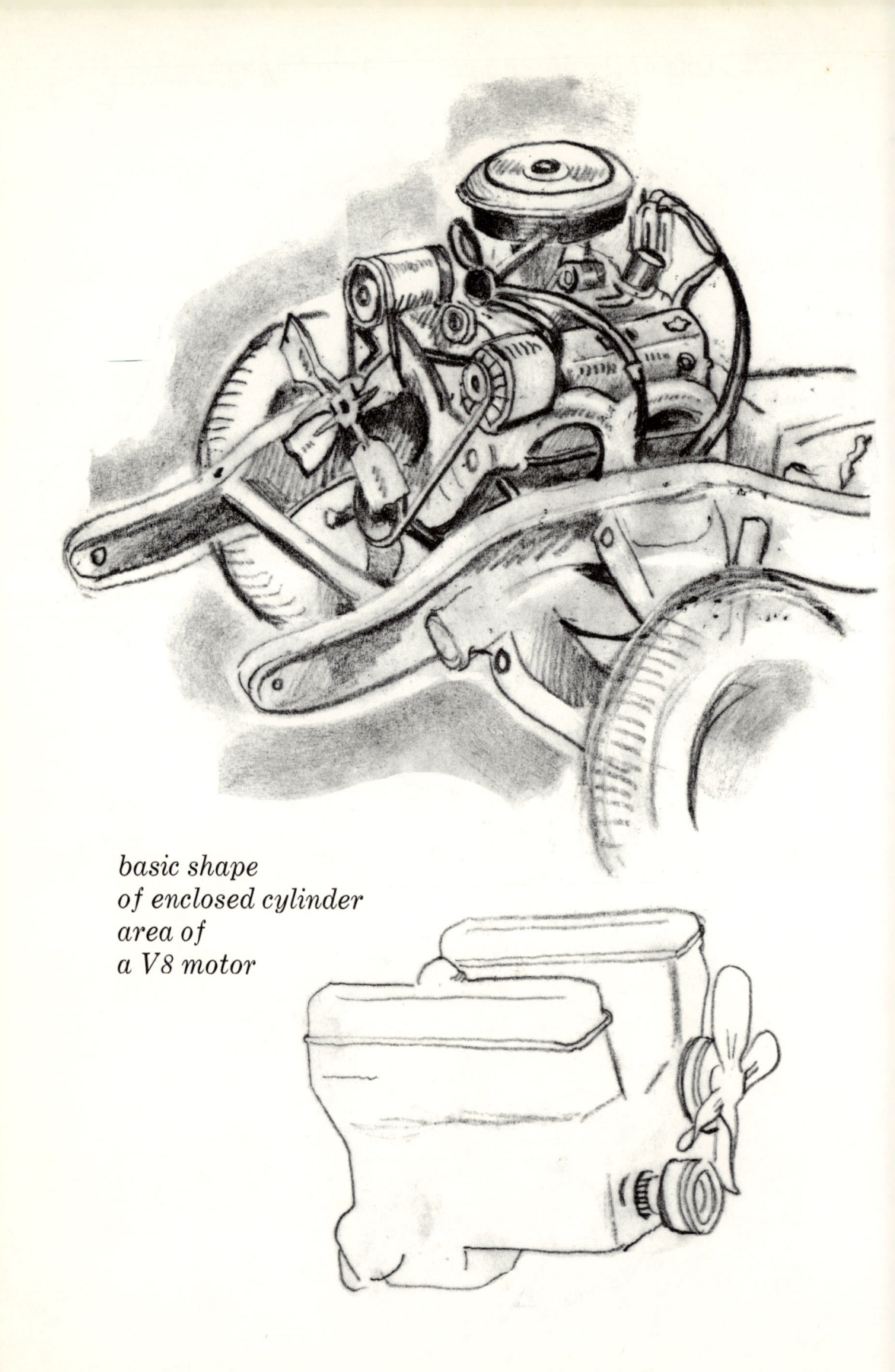

*basic shape
of enclosed cylinder
area of
a V8 motor*

44

outboard motor

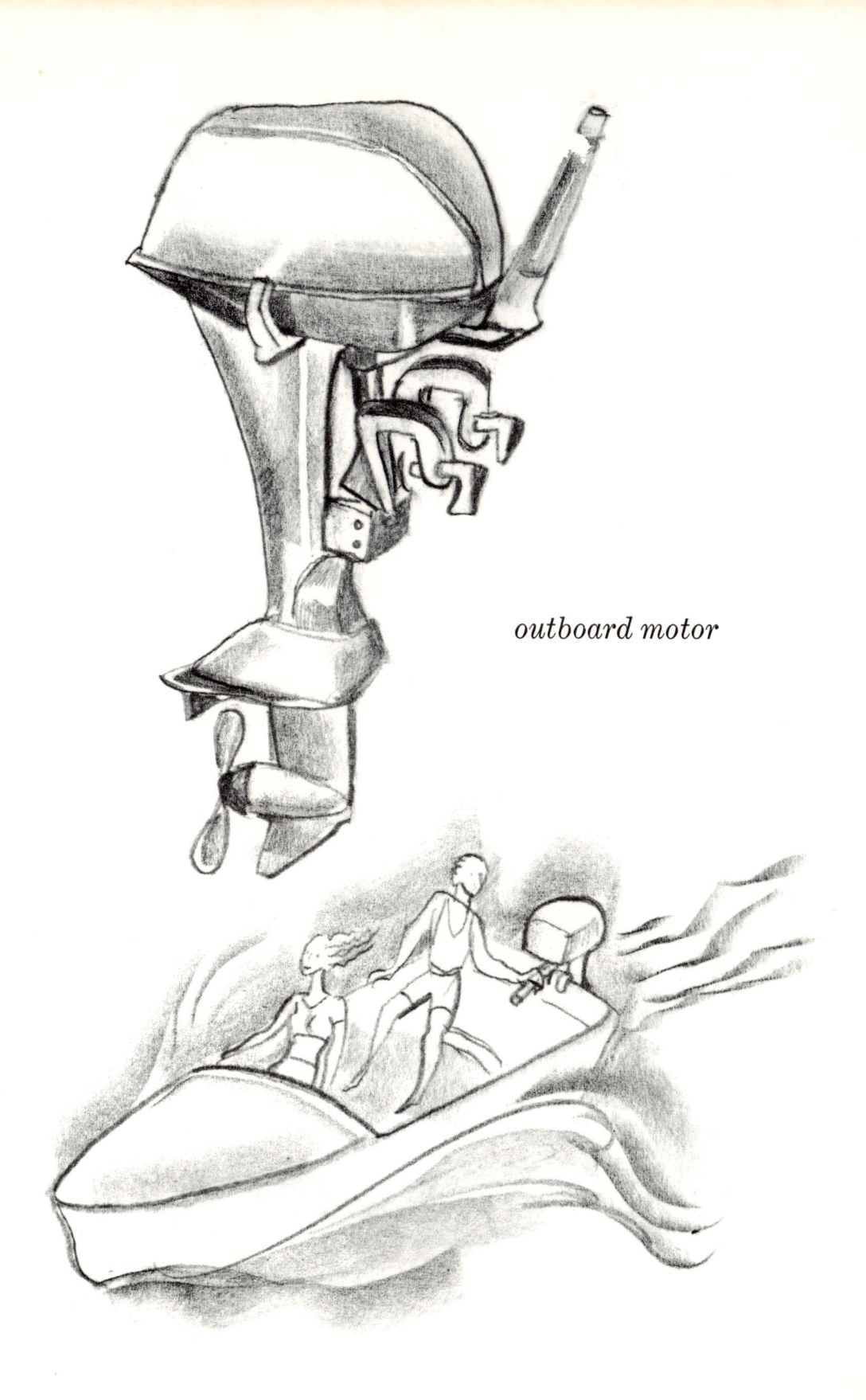

Speed and Power

Everything used by man for his industrial needs is not beautiful. But beauty is not the only thing that interests an artist and makes him want to re-create something on paper or canvas. The great steel mills belching forth their smoke and flames are exciting and dramatic and many artists have used them as subjects for their drawings and paintings.

Although steam locomotives are no longer a part of the daily scene, jet planes, rockets and spaceships have inspired powerful paintings. And the tremendous forces harnessed by scientists in today's space age have influenced many contemporary artists.

When you draw great machines in motion, do not simply copy their outlines and some of the details of their construction. You should try to capture the feeling of *power and movement* they convey by drawing lines of equal power and movement.

Too much detail will make your drawings static and impede the action of even the swiftest racing car. Instead, let your sketches suggest the speed and power of the cars you are depicting rather than attempting any line-for-line reproduction of their outer surfaces.

Machines with enormous power for moving soil have changed the physical appearance of our world and not always for the better, unfortunately. But life has been made easier as a result, and travel and transportation have been greatly facilitated.

Jet Engine

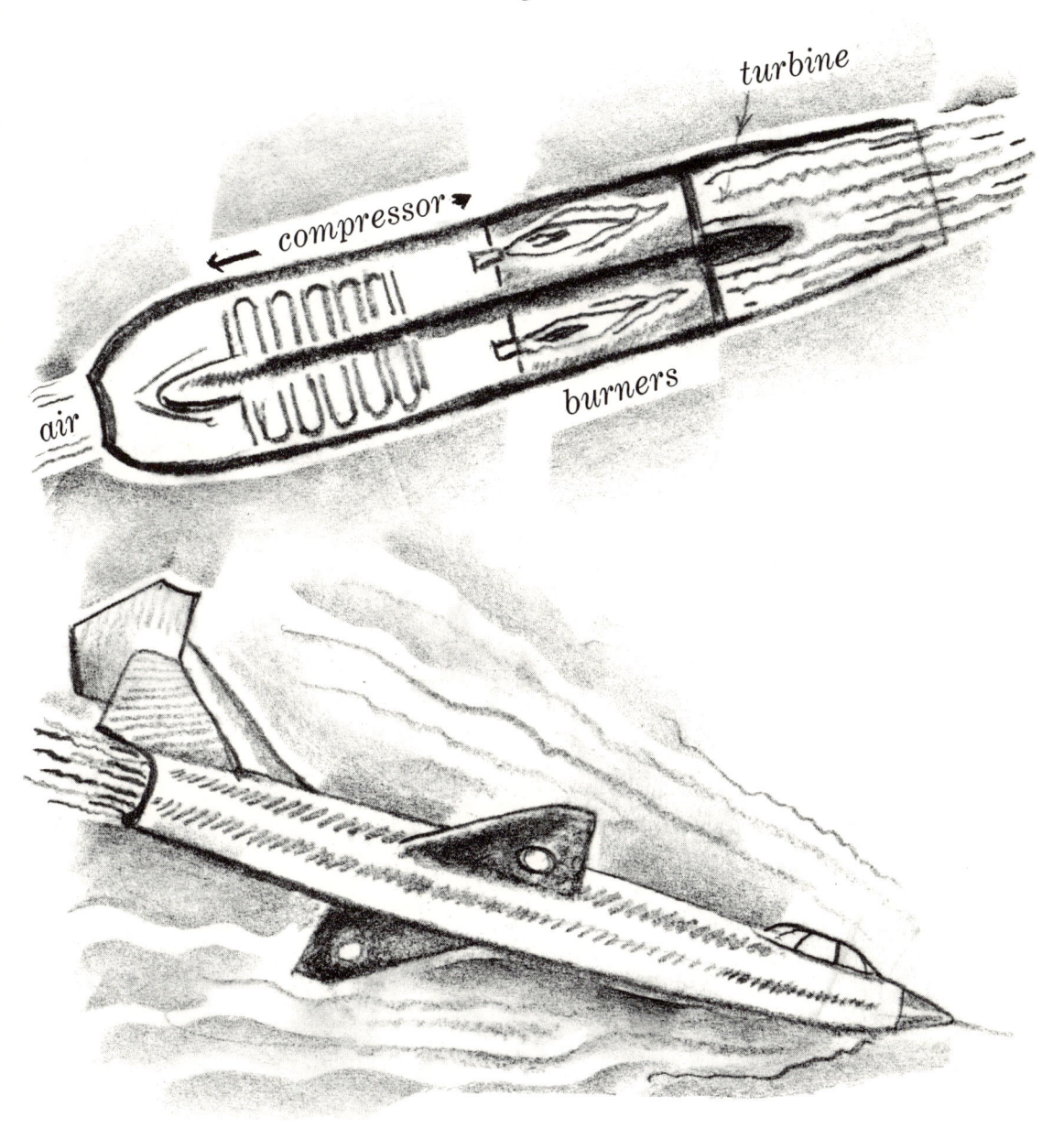

air — compressor — burners — turbine

Jet Plane

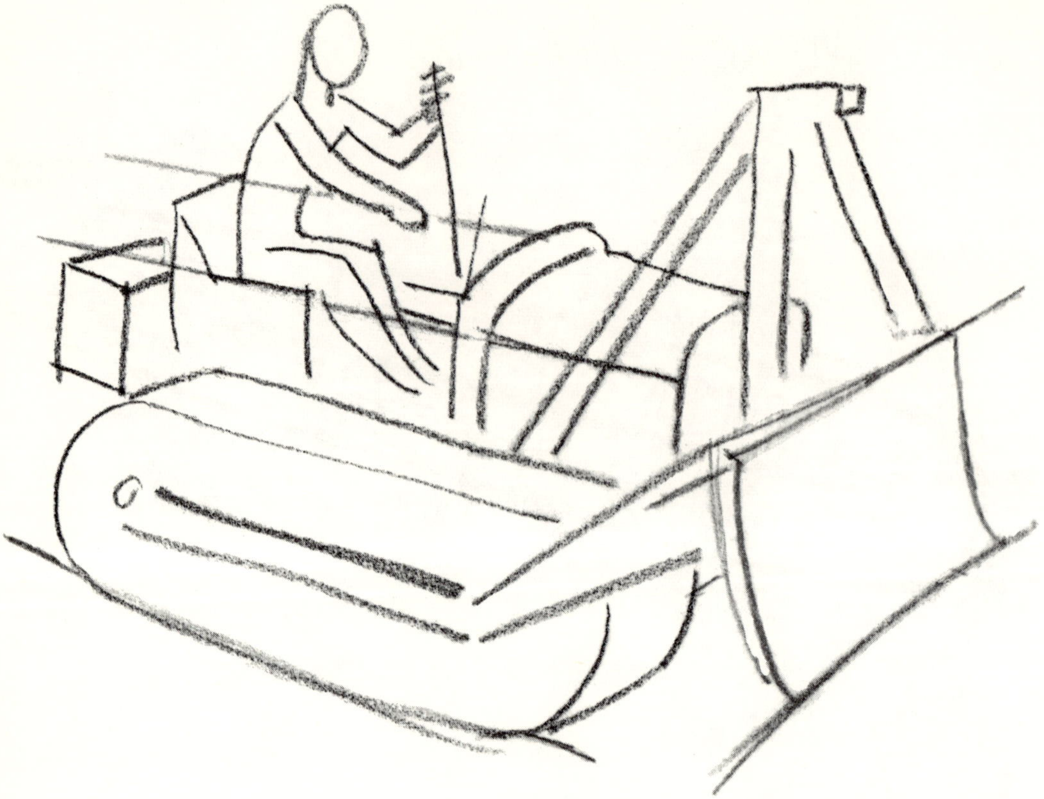

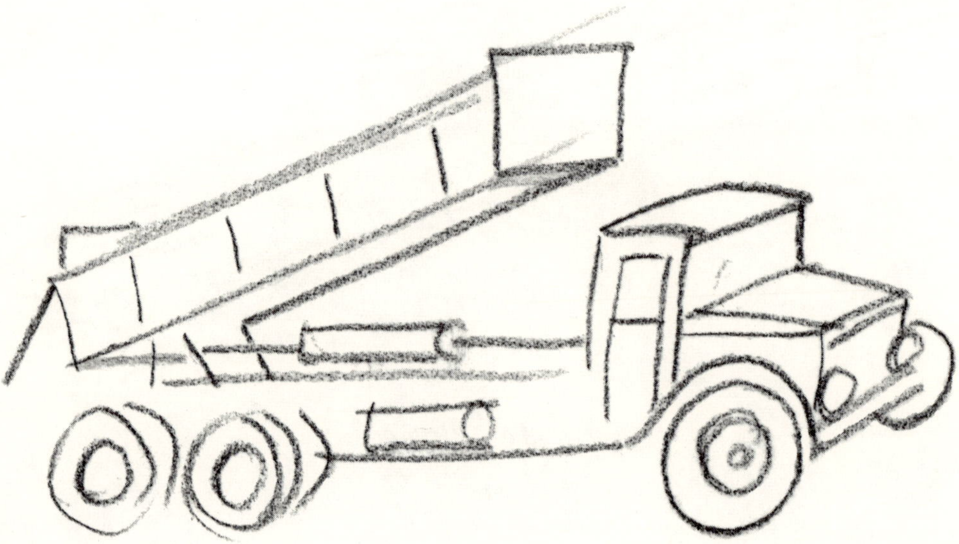

bulldozer

truck with power spill

49

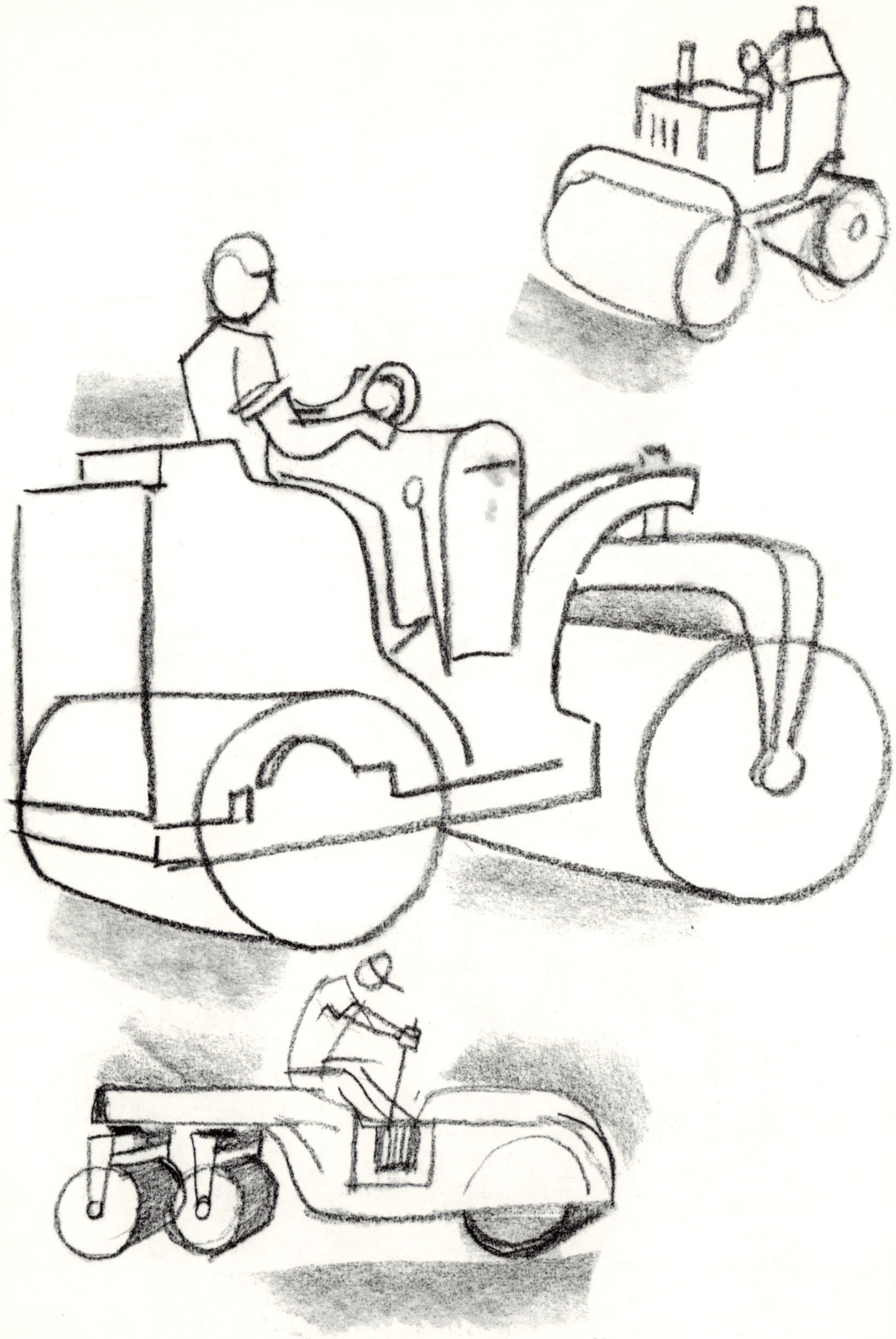

diesel-power roller

52

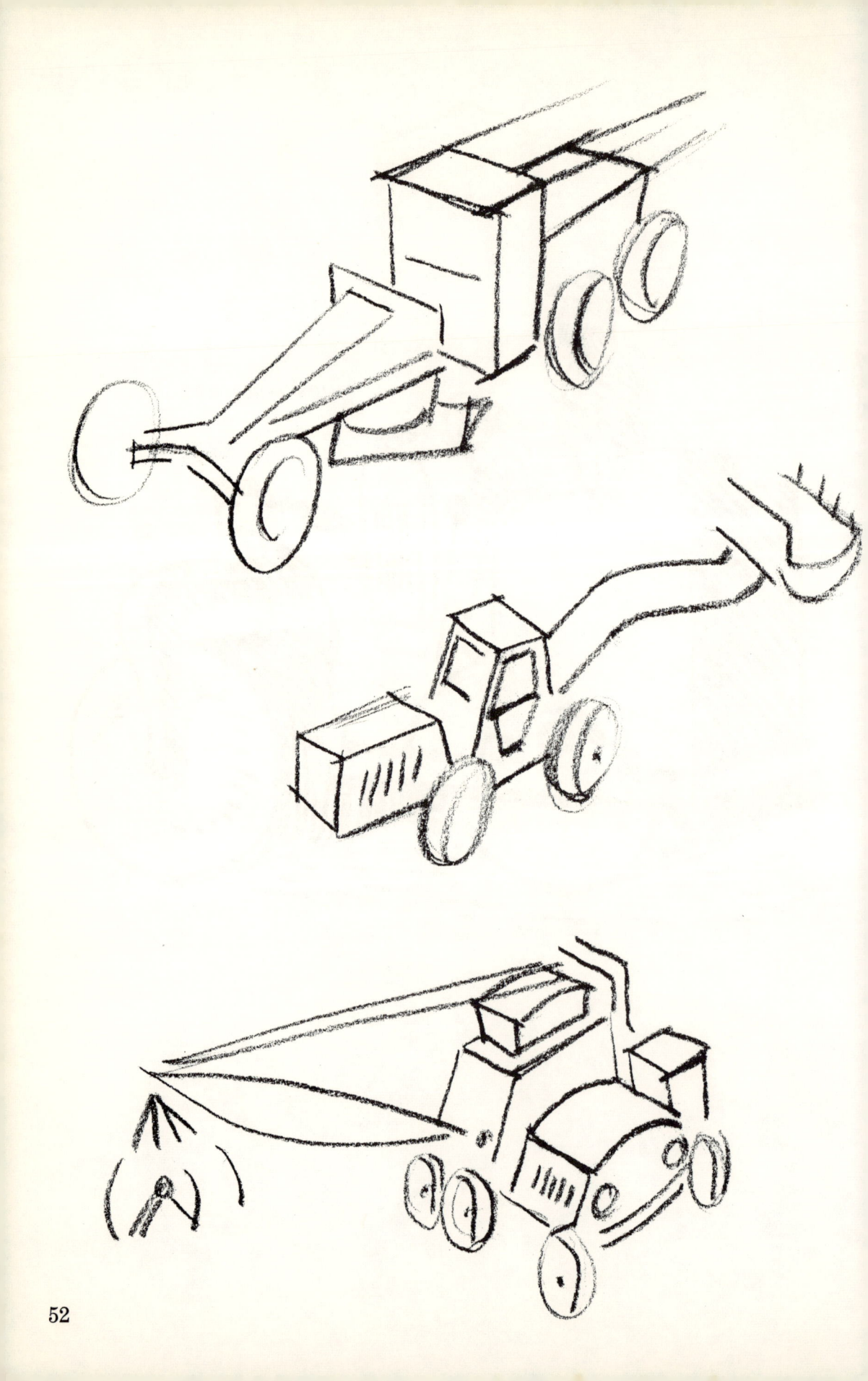

road scraper

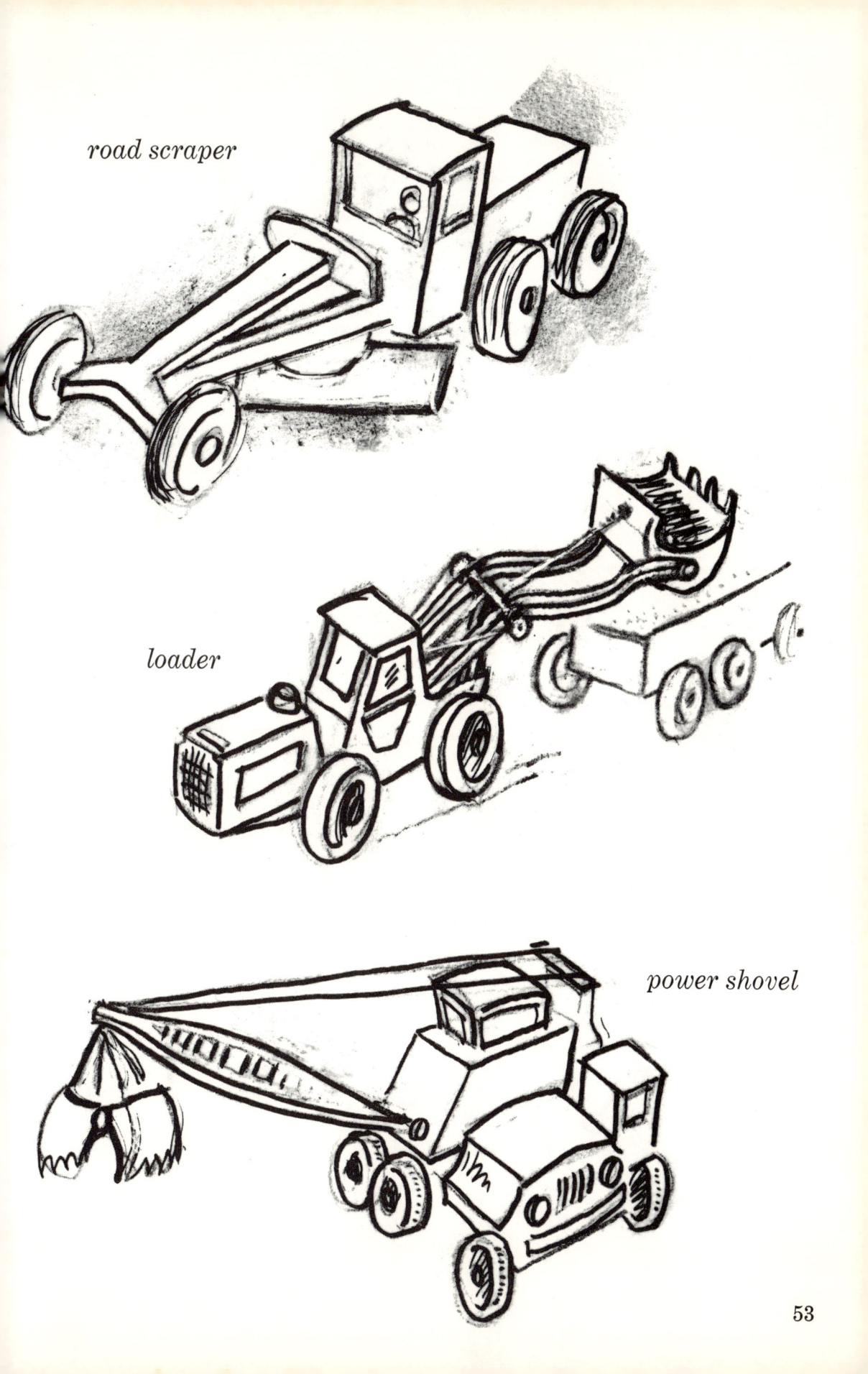

loader

power shovel

tractor

motorcycle

welding metal with oxygen and acetylene flame

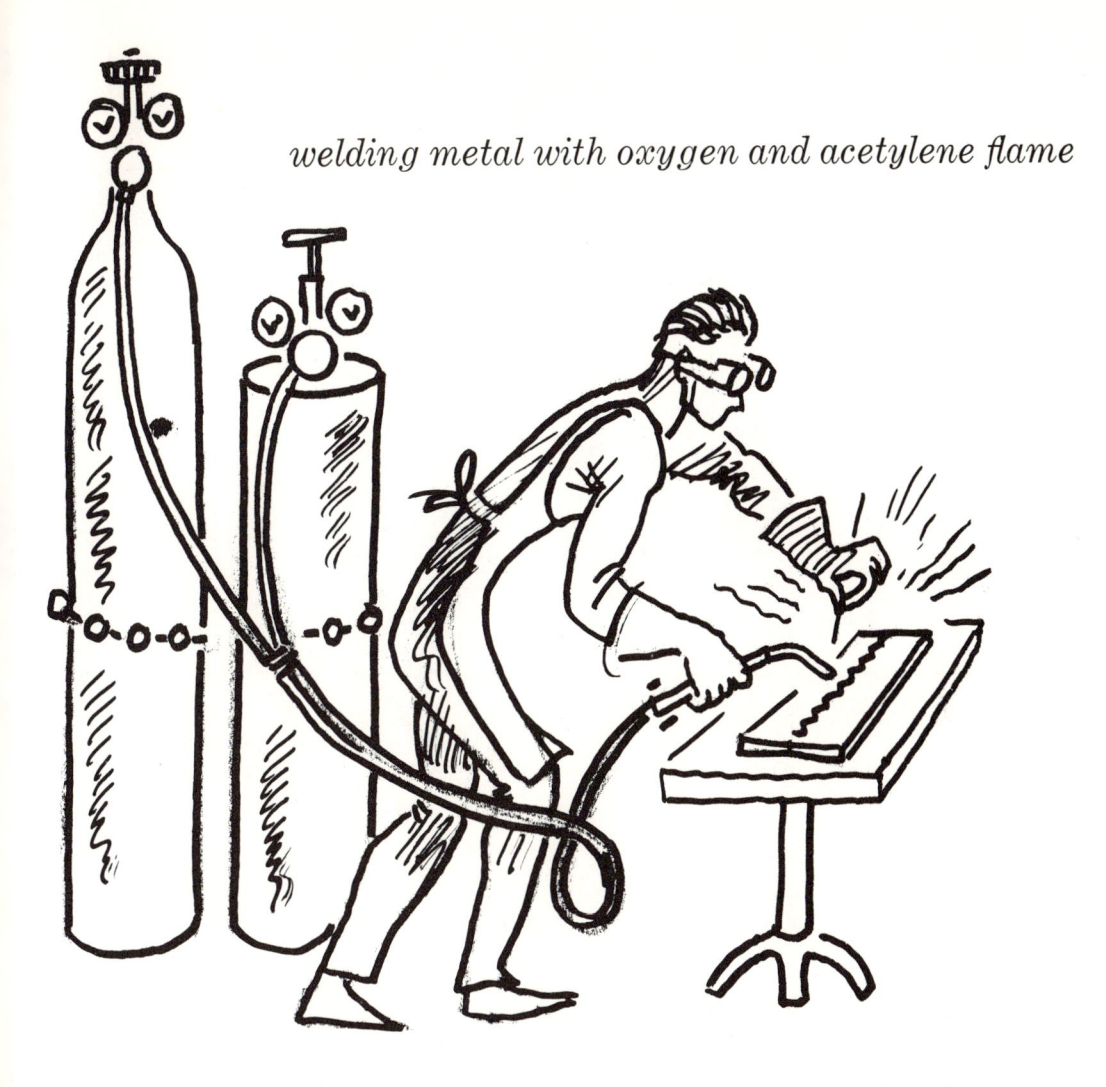

With the increase in the use of iron for weapons, special tools had to be contrived for smelting and forging the metal.

welding torch

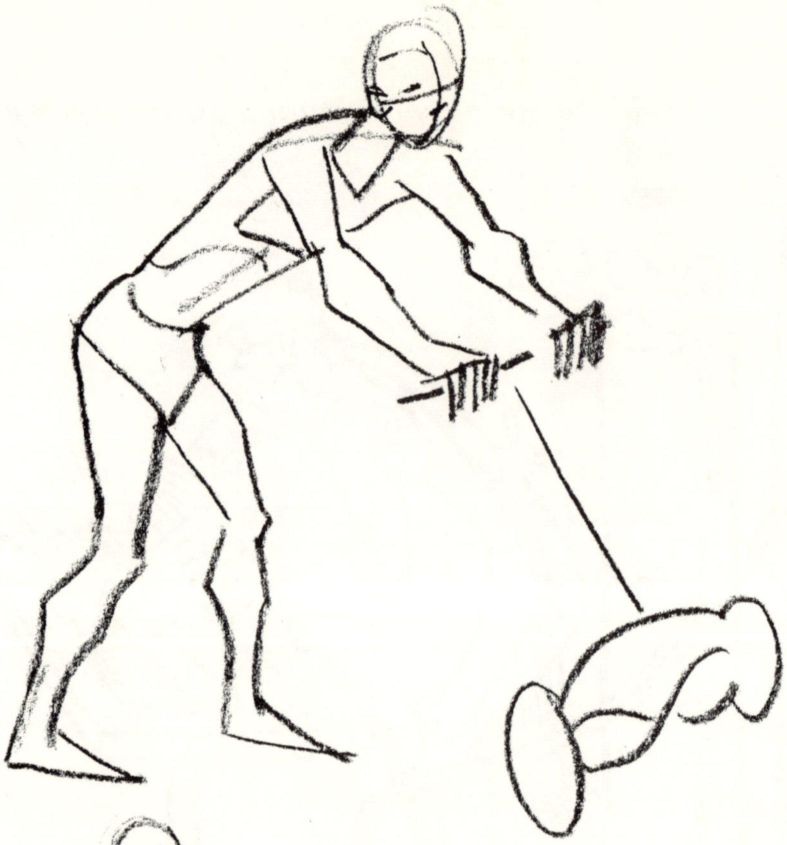

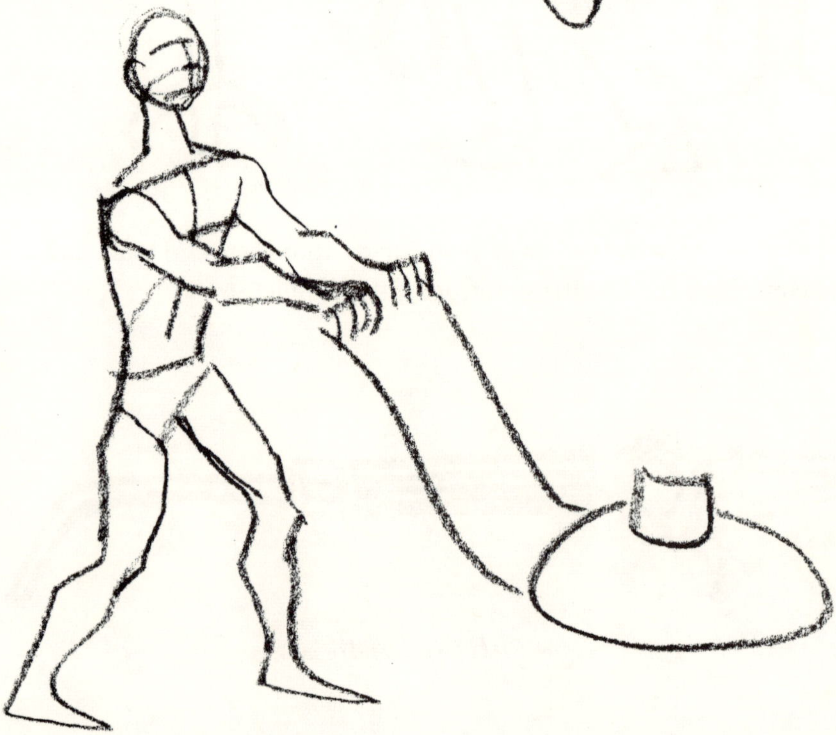

hand mower

power mower

telescope

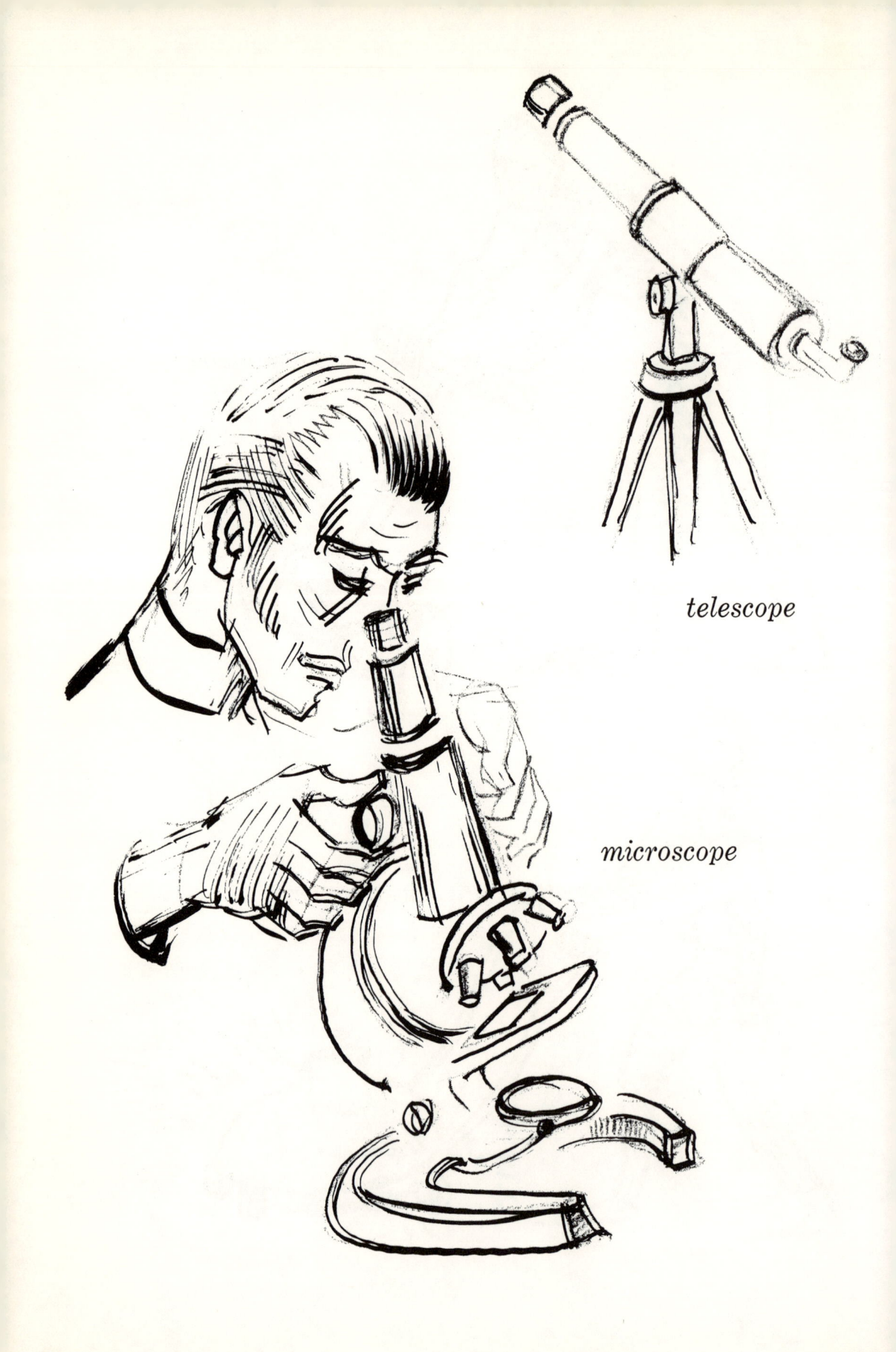

microscope

electric handsaw

Invent Your Own Machinery

You have in your hand a tool with which you can make marvelous creations—a pencil! For a pencil, which has a far greater range than any hand tool made, is a tool in the best sense of the word.

With a pencil, you can draw not only objects you see about you, but you can build machinery conceived by your imagination. The machines you create in your mind and then transfer onto paper may never be built by a manufacturer or be subject to the laws of physics; but if you let your imagination run freely, they can be wonderful *personal* machines whose only function is to stimulate and excite the imagination of those who look at them.

Try to "invent" some of these machines for your own amusement and that of your friends. See what a good artist-inventor you can be!

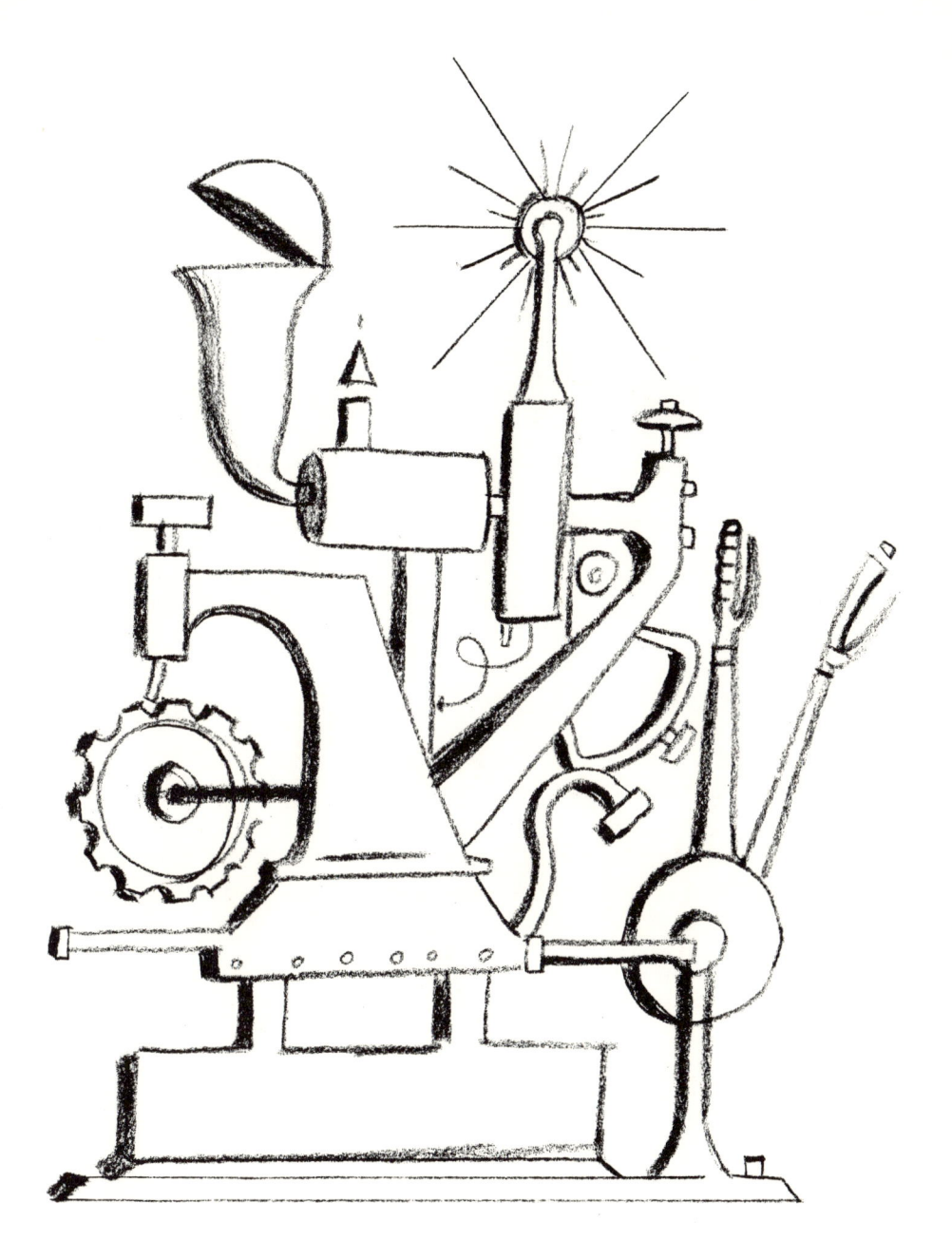

"invented" motor complex

imaginary space craft

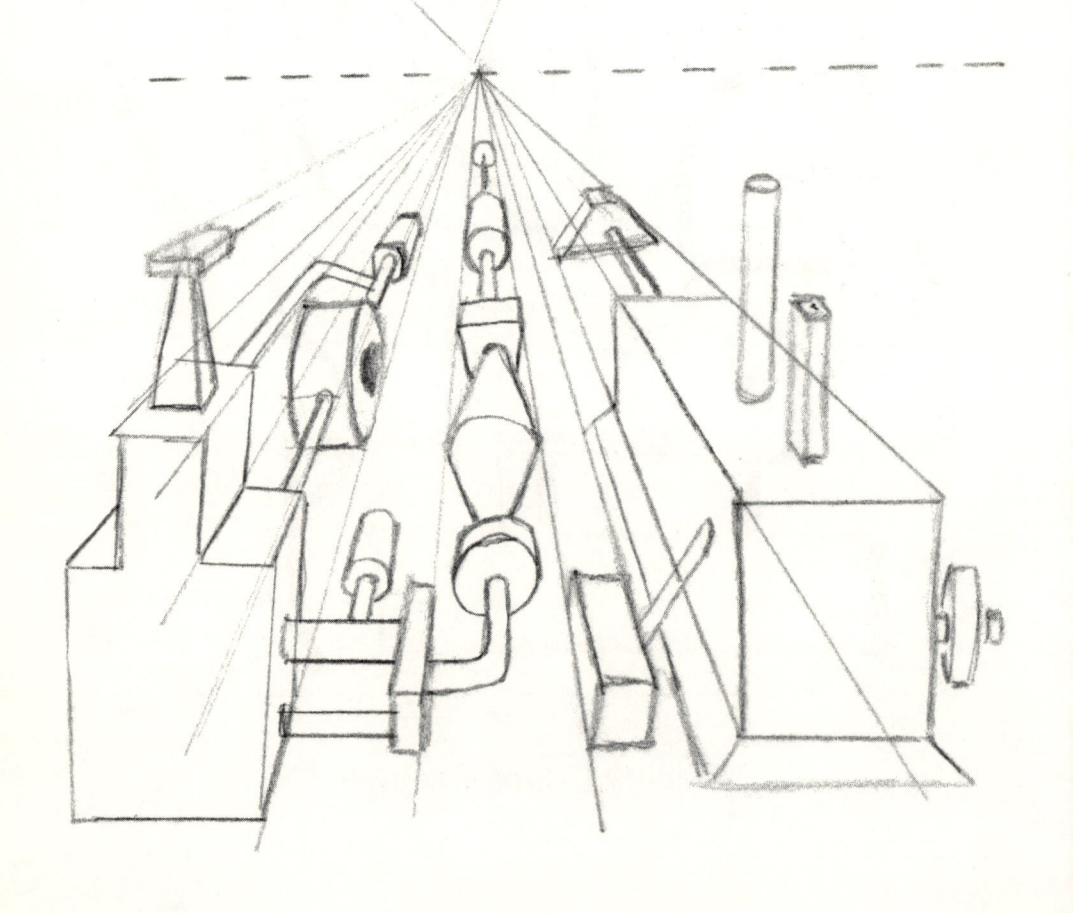

Final Word

It is sincerely hoped that you will follow the suggestions in these pages with interest, pleasure and some profit. Above all, it is hoped that you will continue to practice drawing the subjects described in this book and go on to draw others that especially interest you.

Who knows—you may even become that fine, indispensable contributor to the happiness and enrichment of your community and the world, a fine artist! If you do, you and those who have the privilege of looking at your work will be fortunate indeed. For there is no better or more satisfying life, and the world can never have too many good artists.

But if you only develop the basic skills and knowledge needed to draw for your own pleasure, as a hobby, you will derive a great deal of pleasure from it. And you will perhaps pass along some of that pleasure to others who may see, through your eyes and sketches, what you have created. The important thing is to do your best and utilize whatever talent you may have to the fullest.